The Complete Collaborator

The Complete Collaborator

THE PIANIST AS PARTNER

Martin Katz

OXFORD

UNIVERSITY PRESS

2009

OXFORD
UNIVERSITY PRESS

Oxford University Press, Inc., publishes works that further
Oxford University's objective of excellence
in research, scholarship, and education.

Oxford   New York
Auckland   Cape Town   Dar es Salaam   Hong Kong   Karachi
Kuala Lumpur   Madrid   Melbourne   Mexico City   Nairobi
New Delhi   Shanghai   Taipei   Toronto

With offices in
Argentina   Austria   Brazil   Chile   Czech Republic   France   Greece
Guatemala   Hungary   Italy   Japan   Poland   Portugal   Singapore
South Korea   Switzerland   Thailand   Turkey   Ukraine   Vietnam

Published by Oxford University Press, Inc.
198 Madison Avenue, New York, New York 10016

www.oup.com

Oxford is a registered trademark of Oxford University Press.

Library of Congress Cataloging-in-Publication Data
Katz, Martin, 1945–
The complete collaborator : the pianist as partner / Martin Katz.
p.   cm.
Includes index.
ISBN 978-0-19-536795-9
1. Musical accompaniment. 2. Piano—Performance. I. Title.
MT236.K27   2009
781.47—dc22   2008034250

Recorded audio tracks (marked in text with ●) are available online at www.oup.com/us/thecompletecollaborator
Access with username Music3 and password Book3234

11

Printed in the United States of America
on acid-free paper

Being a professor for nearly twenty-five years, teaching privately, and being engaged for master classes here and abroad—all these activities have enabled me (forced me, actually) to formulate the principles expressed in this book, to define them for myself, to refine them for others, and to articulate them as clearly as I can. Thus I am happy to dedicate this, my opus 1, to my students, past, present, and hopefully future too. I owe all of you so much, and I extend to you my sincerest appreciation. Thanks for keeping me on my toes, but more important, for caring about this crazy specialty as much as I do. You are my inspiration.

And of course, an equal share of gratitude and dedication to Dale. For a first-time author, hurdles and frustrations seem to crop up continually. Patience has never been my forte, and there were many times when I permitted temporary obstacles to ruin my enthusiasm and tempt me to throw in the towel altogether. Dale's encouragement and support have ensured the successful completion of this project. Thank you, D-W.

ACKNOWLEDGMENTS

For years, after classes or concerts, people have remarked, "You must write a book." Well at last I can respond, "I have!" Although I am the author, I've had a great deal of help; books obviously don't write themselves. In no particular order, let me express my appreciation.

My acquiring editor at Oxford, Suzanne Ryan, showed interest in this project immediately, and I am so lucky to have had her on my team.

I am grateful to the Office of the Vice President for Research at the University of Michigan for the very generous grant awarded me. Musical examples, both printed and recorded, would not have been possible without this gift. My colleagues Mary Simoni and Ronald Torrella shepherded me expertly throughout the grant application process and have kept everything on track every step of the way.

Robert Vuichard, himself a fine young composer, was here confined to copying the music of others but never seemed to mind. His expertise proved invaluable to this software-challenged author.

To serve as producer, I drafted my former student Alan Hamilton, a marvelous collaborative pianist himself, and my intuition was more than validated by his fine performance on this project. It's not easy to tell your teacher than he might do better with another take. I also benefited enormously from the recording expertise and experience of Dave Greenspan. Not only did he make me sound good, but he set the fun button at "on" throughout the lengthy process of getting all the examples recorded. His talented students, Piper and both Fosdicks, helped significantly too.

Thanks to Robert Grijalva for providing me with such a well-prepared piano at all hours.

Sarah Frisoff taught me a lot about breathing for flutists, and my dear friend Siri Gottlieb gave gratis Danish diction lessons for Grieg's beautiful love song.

Finally, how can I adequately thank my two partners in crime, soprano Anne Gross and baritone Jesse Blumberg? Recording is never fun or easy, and the difficulty is exacerbated when one is doing only a few measures here or there. These two University of Michigan alumni were such a pleasure to partner, and I'm proud to have their names associated with mine here or anywhere.

Copyrights

The following excerpts are reproduced by permission. All rights reserved.

CONTENTS

About the Companion Web Site
www.oup.com/us/thecompletecollaborator

Oxford has created a password-protected Web site to accompany *The Complete Collaborator*, and the reader is encouraged to take full advantage of it. With the author himself at the piano, more than sixty musical examples illustrate the principles and techniques described in the book. Two accomplished and expressive singers assist him in these informative personal demonstrations.

Reading *and* listening, used together liberally, can enhance the experience immensely. This aural confirmation will validate and guarantee the reader's complete understanding and will quickly encourage added confidence in integrating the new ideas espoused here.

Recorded examples available online are found throughout the text and are signaled with Oxford's symbol ⬤.

MUSICAL EXAMPLES

Italics indicate a recorded example.

Ex.#	Composer	Title
2-1	*Schumann*	*Im wunderschönen Monat Mai*
2-2	*Schubert*	*An die Musik*
2-3	*Fauré*	*Les berceaux*
2-4	*Copland*	*Heart, we will forget him*
2-5	Ives	Two little flowers
2-6	Mozart	Als Luise die Briefe
2-7	*Schubert*	*An die Musik*
2-8	Brahms	Clarinet sonata in f minor, op. 120, #1, i
2-9	*Brahms*	*Botschaft*
2-10	Debussy	C'est l'extase
2-11	*Barber*	*Sure on this shining night*
2-12	*Chopin*	*Nocturne in E-flat, op. 9, #2*
2-13	*Schumann*	*Du Ring an meinem Finger*
2-14	*Strauss*	*Allerseelen*
2-15	*Fauré*	*Nell*
2-16	*Schumann*	*Helft mir, ihr Schwestern*
3-1	*Vaughan Williams*	*Whither must I wander?*
3-2	*Ives*	*The greatest man*
3-3	*Mahler*	*Liebst du um Schönheit*
3-4	*Tosti*	*L'ultimo bacio*
3-5	*Tchaikovsky*	*Средь шумного бала*
3-6	*Barber*	*The daisies*
3-7	*Schubert*	*So lasst mich scheinen, bis ich werde*
3-8	*Brahms*	*Das Mädchen*
3-9	*Strauss*	*Allerseelen*
3-10	*Grieg*	*Jeg elsker Dig!*
3-11	*Obradors*	*Con amores, la mi madre*
3-12	*Rodrigo*	*¿Con qué la lavaré?*

Ex.#	Composer	Title
3-13	Schumann	Violin sonata in a minor, op. 105, ii
3-14	Chopin	Cello sonata, iii
3-15	Beethoven	Violin sonata in c minor, op. 30, #2, ii
4-1	Schumann	Im wunderschönen Monat Mai
4-2	Brahms	Dein blaues Auge
4-3	Schumann	Die Lotosblume
4-4	Schubert	Geheimes
4-5	Schumann	Ich kann's nicht fassen, nicht glauben
4-6	Barber	St. Ita's vision
4-7	Strauss	Ich wollt' ein Sträusslein binden
4-8	Schumann	Aufträge
4-9	Schubert	Der Neugierige
4-10	Wolf	In dem Schatten meiner Locken
4-11	Fauré	Ici-bas
4-12	Duparc	Chanson triste
4-13	Schubert	Am Feierabend
4-14	Debussy	Colloque sentimentale
4-15	Brahms	Vergebliches Ständchen
5-1	Schumann	Aus den hebräischen Gesängen
5-2	Schumann	Zwielicht
5-3	Brahms	Von ewiger Liebe
5-4	Schubert	Suleika
5-5	Schubert	Ganymed
5-6	Wolf	Das verlassene Mägdlein
5-7	Mendelssohn	Die Liebende schreibt
5-8	Strauss	Die Nacht
5-9	Strauss	Das Rosenband
5-10	Schumann	Heiss mich nicht reden
5-11	Britten	Now the leaves are falling fast
5-12	Barber	O boundless, boundless evening
5-13	Strauss	Morgen!
5-14	Musto	Litany
5-15	Rachmaninoff	Не пои, красавица, при мне
5-16	Schumann	Er, der Herrlichste von allen
5-17	Schubert	Gretchen am Spinnrade
5-18	Barber	The desire for hermitage
5-19	Mahler	Die zwei blauen Augen
5-20	Gounod	L'absent
5-21	Poulenc	Nous avons fait la nuit
5-22	Schumann	Waldesgespräch
5-23	Schumann	Nun hast du mir den ersten Schmerz getan
5-24	Schumann	Die alten, bösen Lieder

The Complete Collaborator

ONE

An Introduction:
What Is Collaboration Anyway?

During my high school and college years, and indeed until very recently, I called myself an accompanist and never thought a thing about it. To me, it described everything I do. Nowadays, however, the word "accompanist" has been almost universally replaced. The old title seems to strike many as pejorative, demeaning, or indicative of a lack of self-esteem; as a result, a different word for this specialized art has come into common usage today: collaborative pianist. I still do what I always did, but now, instead of misspelling accompanist (accompianist or acompianist), people can trip over "collaborative" (how many l's and how many b's are there anyway?). The Latin roots of this word are patently obvious; "with" and "work" are found in equal measure here, and indeed, as collaborators, we work with others. As the reader will come to see, we are speaking of the largest meanings of both these root words.

Whatever we may call this art, it is not the simplest way to make music, although when all is said and done, it may be the most fulfilling. It has certainly been that for me. Of immediate concern, however, is the notion that collaboration is merely rhythmic synchronization, vertical alignment, if you will, along with the care not to play too loudly. To be sure, both perfect ensemble and good balance with one's partners are essential—I will devote quite a bit of space to both these subjects—but they are only a small part of the big picture of collaboration, and perhaps the least imaginative of all our jobs. A quick glance at the chapters that follow will give some idea of the myriad tasks facing any accomplished collaborator. Some of these challenges demand our physical understanding of how our partners feel; others are entirely subjective as we wordlessly tell stories or emotionally manipulate our partners and our audience. We are fourfold custodians: We guard and maintain the composer's wishes, the poet's requirements as the composer saw them, our partners' emotional and physical needs, and finally, of course, our own needs as well. I believe passionately in this quadruple responsibility, and I will try to articulate here what my many years of experience have taught me, experience not only on the concert stage, in the recording studio, and in rehearsal, but also as a teacher of this specialized way of thinking and playing—collaborative piano in its largest sense.

If I did not believe all of this could be calculated and organized, I would not have set out to write this text in the first place. Indeed, I know that it can be analyzed and codified and finally articulated in order to impart it to others, because I have done so. Previous generations of pianists were advised that collaborative talent was a kind of innate radar; one was born with it or not, period. In truth, after all of the ideas presented herein have been digested and implemented, 10 percent of a collaborator's success might still be attributed to an arcane, mystical ability to intuit what on earth one's partner might do next. If it exists, that small percentage cannot be verbalized or taught, and thus cannot be examined in this or any other text. It can only be appreciated and used to add icing to the cake. In this text, I much prefer to offer objective (well, perhaps occasionally subjective) guidance that can give a pianist almost all the tools required to achieve a complete fusion with his or her partner.

It will be probably be immediately apparent that this text is directed chiefly at collaborative pianists, those attracted to this specialized field, those seeking to improve, or perhaps those gifted collaborators who already excel at this way of making music but who have never articulated to themselves or to others what it is exactly that works so well. Perhaps the reader will need to teach collaboration at some point; more and more schools are adding courses in ensemble playing as its worth becomes less taken for granted and more appreciated. But informed collaboration need not be reserved for the professional pianist or graduate music student; I would hope that interested amateurs and curious novices might also be intrigued by what is discussed here, and that their performances too might profit from new information or new ways of expressing established ideas or instincts. The interested, sensitive listener who reads this text may also develop an increased appreciation for all that collaborators must do. The musical examples I have chosen are all from the standard repertoire, and the technical language, it is hoped, will be familiar and friendly.

Let me digress just a moment: To absolve myself of sexism from the outset, I will alternate between using "he" and "she" when referring to the performers throughout this book, in order to avoid the necessity of endlessly repeating cumbersome additional words. For fun, I will juggle the pronouns for both pianists and soloists as I proceed from chapter to chapter. If I were writing this as few as thirty years ago, I would not have allowed myself this shortcut; at that time, so few women were able to make careers in this field—for nothing but ridiculous reasons—that I would have felt it to be my mission to insist on always mentioning both genders. Females were found at the keyboard occasionally as behind-the-scene coaches perhaps, but on the stage and in public, they appeared all too rarely. My own teacher, Gwendolyn Koldofsky, managed to beat this bias against serious odds, but even as late as 1964 no less a celebrity than Marilyn Horne had to stubbornly insist on having Koldofsky with her on stage for her New York recital debut. Today, however, this absurd prejudice and unjustifiable tradition have given way to impartial good sense, and I am happy to see concert stages, rehearsal halls, coaching studios and music schools populated with men and women collaborators in equal numbers. I can thereby benefit in this text and leapfrog from gender to gender in every other chapter.

I hope that once the techniques and ideas discussed here have been understood and correctly implemented, they will disappear into the fabric of a performance. The finished product will not allow for separating the partners from one another. Perhaps another informed and aware collaborative pianist might discern the mechanics at work, but certainly no one else should be able to do so. Sometimes even the singer or instrumentalist being partnered will be unaware of all that is transpiring (or not!) underneath and around him, but he will somehow sense that he is more (or less!) comfortable in so many ways, and therefore more available for expression than ever before. To the audience and the soloist, this performance will seem natural, believable, organic, and it will shine with a physical and emotional inevitability.

Let us take to heart the words of Richard Strauss's immortal creation, the Marschallin, as she tells us in act one:

> *Doch in dem "Wie" liegt der grosse Unterschied.*
> But it is in the "How" that all the difference lies.

Two

Breathing and Singing

The primary building block of successful collaboration is surely the breath. If you are to read only a single chapter of this book, please make it this one! Like me, many of my esteemed colleagues in collaboration admit to being secret would-be singers. It can be no accident then, that the voices and instruments we all accompany should enjoy the fruits of our vicarious but utterly complete physical identification where breathing is concerned. Any musician benefits from singing and, of necessity, breathing, but particularly those for whom air is *not* required to make the instrument work. A conductor, a violinist, an organist, and we hard-working pianists can play for hours at a time without taking a breath, and that is precisely the problem. For the pianist, singing and breathing are beyond crucial. Ignorance of this issue might limit a solo pianist's success somewhat, but for an accompanist it would be a disaster. Whether it be a physical necessity or an artistic choice, nothing approaches the importance of breathing in the quest for true collaboration.

I have never (well, almost never) stepped onto a stage or even into a rehearsal without being able to sing the soloist's music and play my own part simultaneously. If I have not yet achieved this coordination, then I know without a doubt that I am not ready to collaborate with another on this piece. Doing this may require very little practice, perhaps, for Barber's "A nun takes the veil" or Beethoven's "Ich liebe dich," or I may be facing endless hours to master the multi-tasking of Strauss's "Cäcilie" or Debussy's "Mandoline." All these practice hours must occur *before* we meet with our partners. Regardless of the difficulty involved, my credo is: If you can't sing it, you can't play it! By singing, I do not mean murmuring, whispering, or mouthing words to avoid embarrassment; I am speaking of truly using and enjoying our own voices, and as a result, requiring fuel in the form of breaths. No one would require a collaborative pianist to have a beautiful tone; we need only lungs, a mouth, and, most important, the permission we give ourselves to feel foolish and vulnerable. Then and only then can we begin to identify with our partners and know how to handle various breathing issues.

Before we proceed with analyzing breath situations, it is necessary to acknowledge and accept as axiomatic that the ongoing progress of the music is our ultimate goal. Getting from the first note to the last is the job at hand. If the keyboard part has the moving notes, which is most often the case, this crucial responsibility is literally in our hands. If we prevent this progress, we can do so only when all other options have been eliminated or if a very unusual and striking effect is appropriate.

Once we have experienced singing a piece ourselves, it is an easy task to classify each breath the soloist takes as belonging to one of three categories.

Type I: Nothing *Need* Be Done

This situation occurs when the soloist can inhale adequately, execute a phrase, finish the phrase in a polished manner, inhale again, and enter for the next phrase—accomplishing all of this without disturbing the ongoing flow and tempo of the piece. In this situation, there is enough time after the last note of a phrase to breathe. There may or may not be a printed rest between the phrases; the last note of the first phrase may need to be shortened, but what remains has enough length and polish to be deemed acceptable. Obviously, it is a given that the very first phrase of any piece falls into this category.

What does this situation require of the pianist? Nothing at all. Being the guardian of the music's progress, and recognizing this situation, the pianist has no worries beyond playing well. Later we will deal with telegraphing to the soloist *how* to reenter, but here we are speaking only of *when* to do so. As always, when our partner is absent—even momentarily—we may choose to play with a bit more sound, or more ego, for we are briefly the only game in town, but to reiterate, a pianist with no collaborative training or experience can remove this type of breath from his list of concerns. He continues to play normally, the soloist exits artistically, breathes, and reenters without difficulty, and the music never stops.

Here are some examples of this type of breath. In all the musical examples that follow, breaths are indicated with check marks in both voice and piano parts. As you listen to the recorded examples, note how I simply play the piano part, rhythmically disregarding the singer's entrances and exits. Nothing need be done by me.

Throughout the text, a 🌀 indicates a recorded example:

EXAMPLE 2-1 Schumann, "Im wunderschönen Monat Mai"

EXAMPLE 2-2 Schubert, "An die Musik"

EXAMPLE 2-3 Fauré, "Les berceaux"

EXAMPLE 2-4 Copland, "Heart, we will forget him"

EXAMPLE 2-5 Ives, "Two little flowers"

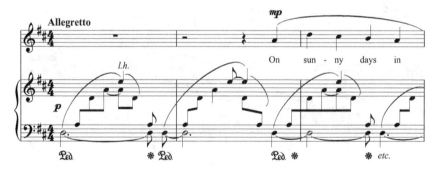

EXAMPLE 2-5 Continued

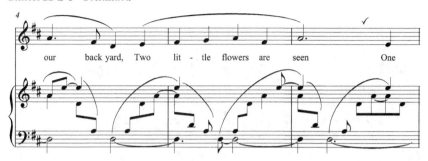

our   back yard,   Two   lit - tle   flowers   are   seen   One

Type 2: Nothing *Can* Be Done; There Are No Options

Easily identifiable, this situation exists when the soloist breathes, but cannot re-enter in tempo, *and* the accompaniment is in rhythmic unison with the voice. The pianist has no notes to himself, only the same rhythmic impulses that the soloist has at her disposal. Thus, whether it occurs out of physical necessity or as a choice based on text or a theatrical coup, the soloist's breath stops the piece cold in its tracks. This might be seen as the least musical or the most theatrical of situations, and fortunately it is the least frequently encountered of the three breath types, since the ongoing flow of the music is completely destroyed momentarily.

Again, this requires nothing from the pianist beyond identification of the type of breath involved plus avid listening. There is nothing in the physical execution of the keyboard part that can disguise this potentially awkward moment. This is what I referred to in chapter 1 as the legal minimum for vertical alignment; the pianist and indeed the composition itself are the hostages of the soloist's need to breathe.

And yet it is our business as collaborators to affirm and justify this kind of stop in the music's flow. We do not ordinarily stop our sound to match the soloist's silence, but wait willingly, with enough tone on our poor decaying piano, while the soloist does what is necessary. No sense of frustration or a resentful "Must you really breathe here?" should be detected in the pianist's performance. We enthusiastically second the motion, as it were, and create a sense of permission to breathe without apologies, and always with commitment and artistry. We have no other options here.

Some examples of type 2:

EXAMPLE 2-6 Mozart, "Als Luise die Briefe"

brennt lan - ge noch viel - leicht   in mir, brennt lan - ge noch viel - leicht in mir.

EXAMPLE 2-7 Schubert, "An die Musik"

du hol - de   Kunst,___ ich dan - ke dir!

EXAMPLE 2-8 Brahms, Clarinet sonata in f minor, op. 120, #1, i

EXAMPLE 2-9 Brahms, "Botschaft"

EXAMPLE 2-10 Debussy, "C'est l'extase"

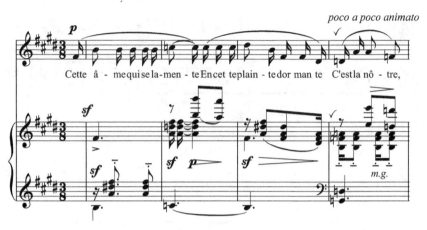

EXAMPLE 2-11 Barber, "Sure on this shining night"

Before proceeding, I would emphasize again that with these first two categories of breaths, very little is required of the pianist. A piano soloist would not require much additional information or experience to handle these breaths expertly, nor would this chapter be as crucial as I have stated. It is in the third category that true understanding of and physical identification with the soloist shows the pianist's aptitude and talent for collaboration. I would venture to state that of all the techniques discussed in this text, this is the most important to be understood and mastered. It is the basis of everything.

Type 3: Permit Breath and Preserve Flow

Having sung the piece himself, the pianist has now identified those phrases where exit and reentry cannot be accomplished in tempo, but the difference between this type 3 breath and type 2 could not be more significant: In this third situation, there is intervening material in the keyboard part during the absence of the soloist. It may be but a single note, a few chords, or perhaps an elaborate arpeggio—this depends on the pattern and texture the composer has invented for the piano— but it gives us the tools to preserve the flow of the music (type 2 does not, remember) and *at the same time* allows the singer to feel permission to fill her tank without apology. Here, the music seems never to stop.

One hears so many performances in which uninformed but well-meaning pianists cope with this situation gracelessly. These less than ideal solutions are variously described as "ritard," "spread," "expand," or perhaps "stretch." Worst of all is a pianist playing in tempo to the end of his intervening material and then simply waiting for the reentry of his partner—not dissimilar to walking straight into a wall, recovering, and proceeding in a different direction. All of these undesirable methods of handling type 3 breaths maintain the vertical alignment, but oh, how the music's flow and integrity are compromised! I believe a far more musical solution is available, one that readily acknowledges the soloist's need for breath *and* maintains the progress of the music, hence my title for this technique: Permit and Preserve, which, unfortunately, sounds very much like a recruiting slogan for the military.

The pianist chooses a point in the accompaniment after the soloist's last note and before the first note for her next phrase. Having chosen this point, the pianist phrases here—earlier than his partner—and proceeds in tempo. Extra time is thus taken by the pianist, but that extra time is *not vertically aligned* with where the soloist is taking her own extra time to breathe. When I suggest that the pianist phrase somewhere in the intervening material, I do not mean to suggest for a moment that the composer's articulation directions are to be changed; I mean only that the pianist's timing can be altered. This can even be done beautifully with only one intervening note, which is sometimes all we have.

It is essential that this method *not* be combined with the unenlightened methods I cited earlier. If the pianist phrased during the intervening material as I am suggesting, and *also* ritarded or expanded that same material, more time than required would be added to the flow of the music, and a very artificial, inorganic, and inappropriate elasticity would result. Singers, winds, and brass players breathe involuntarily when they are out of air, and this physiological and emotional desire to reenter is aided and abetted when the intervening piano part is flowing in tempo. Thus both halves of the instructions for this type of breath are equally crucial: phrase early *and* proceed in tempo, permit the breath, and preserve the flow. Omitting either is helping neither soloist nor composer.

All of the foregoing is perhaps more easily understood with musical examples:

EXAMPLE 2-12 Chopin, Nocturne in E-flat, op. 9, #2

To demonstrate this technique, let us consider the right hand to be the breathing soloist here, and the left hand the accompanist. In order to finish the first phrase gracefully, breathe, and reenter with the second phrase's pickup note, a bit of extra, out-of-tempo time is required. How do I know this? I have sung it myself and felt it in my own body. This is not an intellectual judgment; it is rooted in physicality. An eighth note is not quite sufficient for an expressive soloist and might cause the singer to end the first phrase crudely or abruptly. The pianist phrases before the eleventh left-hand note in the bar and proceeds in tempo. Just a bit of extra time is now acquired, the right hand "breathes" before the twelfth note in the bar, and the music seems never to stop.

Conversely, an uninformed handling of this situation would have the pianist phrasing *after* the eleventh note and waiting for his partner to be ready to continue. Try this. You will surely hear the music stop dead in its tracks! This is not collaboration; this is not permission to breathe; nothing about this sounds natural. This might be considered triage, but certainly not a remedy.

Now some examples from the *real* vocal literature:

EXAMPLE 2-13 Schumann, "Du Ring an meinem Finger"

There is but one intervening note between "Finger" and "mein" for the pianist, but it is enough. The pianist phrases before this sixth note in the bar, proceeds in tempo, and the singer, now full of air, is swept back into the song.

EXAMPLE 2-14 Strauss, "Allerseelen"

Just as with the first example, the pianist here phrases before the sixth note in this bar and proceeds in tempo. When a pianist uses this technique, he should avoid apologizing for doing so; do not hide your collaborative insight—let its benefits be heard!

● EXAMPLE 2-15 Fauré, "Nell"

This is a much more excited song, with a shimmering accompaniment that must remain so, always horizontal and linear in attitude. In this example the pianist has three intervening notes between the singer's exit and her reentry. It would be acceptable for the pianist to phrase before the third or fourth sixteenth note in beat three, but the song's enthusiasm would be slightly reduced. I would therefore suggest the best choice to be phrasing before the second note in beat three, and of course, as always, proceeding in tempo.

EXAMPLE 2-16 Schumann, "Helft mir, ihr Schwestern"

EXAMPLE 2-16 Continued

We have an even more excited example here—it is close to wedding vow time after all! This song taxes any singer's breathing, and after only four measures she will be winded, needing significant extra out-of-tempo time to inhale. Again, as with the Fauré example above, I would suggest the earliest of the possible legal phrasing options for the pianist. This choice not only affords the singer enough time, but preserves the joyous hyperactive atmosphere of this particular song.

It is worth pointing out that a type 2 breath never changes in terms of the pianist's responsibilities. We cannot proceed ahead of our partner *ever!* However with types 1 and 3, the tempo chosen for the piece has everything to do with its breath type. A higher metronome mark turns a type 1 into a type 3, while with a slower tempo a type 3 may morph back into its easier cousin, type 1. Again, the only truly guaranteed way for the pianist to categorize breathing situations and to know how to behave, is—you guessed it—singing! Your own singing! It is always the surefire passport to your most musical decisions.

A final caveat about breathing is in order here—delivered much too late, I fear: I would warn collaborative pianists against telling their partners about the type 3 breath situation and how it is to be handled. All of the suggestions I have made are predicated on natural, involuntary, unselfconscious breathing by the soloist. Too much information about what we are doing at the keyboard while breaths are taken can ruin everything. Soloists will begin to think too much about how and when they breathe, the natural process will be ruined, and this problem will be impossible to correct ever again. Pianists, say not a word! When your partners compliment you on how easily they breathe with you as their collaborator, let them believe it is radar, or sheer luck, or magic of the spheres, and something of which you yourself are not even aware. As far as your partners are concerned, this chapter never happened!

THREE

The Word Is the Thing

Doch kommt das Wort und fasst es
Yet the word comes and seizes it

After more than forty years of professional work as a collaborator, probably the compliment I have savored most is still with me: "Oh, Mr. Katz, I just loved your performance. You really played the *words!*"

Apart from a handful of concert vocalises, any collaboration with a singer means dealing with language. In our pursuit of perfect ensemble and fusion with our partner, we cannot proceed very far down the road without words entering the picture. After all, it is the text that probably inspired the composer in the first place, and it is the text that serves as the conduit for the feelings to be expressed. Words are also a lot of fun, but that's beside the point.

By the way, collaborative pianists working primarily with instruments might think themselves immune from the issues raised in this chapter, but as we shall see, there are instrumental moments which share many of the same concerns found in the vocal repertoire.

A collaborative pianist working with voices need not be fluent in a foreign language, but the more acquaintance she has with the sounds and mechanics of a language, the easier the ensemble tasks become. I recall, in the first years of my own career, feeling totally comfortable with Western European languages, but when accompanying singers in Russian and Czech repertoire, having no idea what the next sound would be nor whether it was an important word. I can only liken the experience to driving a car at rush hour with one's eyes closed—and in front of an audience!

Diction

There are two aspects to achieving perfect ensemble with texted music, and the first and more easily understood is the sound of each syllable. We cannot begin to speak of meaning or expressive options until we are sure of our vertical alignment—the legal minimum for ensemble appears again—and text plays a crucial role in this quest. It is essential to accept the notion that *the vowel sound is the music*, not the consonant or consonants that may initiate that syllable. Even when the preceding consonant is expressive or voiced, it is not the official attack of the note in question. As collaborators committed to perfect ensemble, our own notes must be synchronized precisely with those of our partners, and thus we always play on the vowel sound, never before it.

There are also instrumental, non-texted equivalents of this doctrine. For example, any string chord that cannot be played in a single impulse will require the same collaborative technique as I am describing here for vowels that cannot be reached perfectly in tempo. Always synchronize with the last impulse played. Be sure to read about this device in more detail in chapter 11. If this concept of playing on the vowel sound or the completion of the instrumental chord is not respected, the result will be the distinct impression that the pianist is playing significantly ahead of her partner.

The plot thickens with languages in which multiple consonants are frequently found in succession and used for expression. Words also have a nasty habit of meeting each other, and, here too, the result is clusters of consonants. Pronounce these pairs of words as a great actor would, clearly and expressively, and notice how delayed the second vowel sound is:

> that str<u>a</u>wberry
> sick gl<u>ea</u>m
> strange m<u>u</u>sic

This delayed vowel may be the result of an articulation difficulty or an expressive choice by the singer. In almost every language one can lengthen and exploit an initial consonant to enhance the meaning of a word. Again, some examples:

> <u>Sh</u>ut up!
> I <u>l</u>oathe you!
> Muss ich <u>w</u>einen <u>b</u>itterlich
> T'amo <u>t</u>anto (NB: the second T is treated as a double TT)
> Marcher <u>d</u>roit

If a pianist has a note to be synchronized with the second of any of these vowel pairs in the first list above, or with the expressive examples in the second list, it would be necessary to delay the piano's attack until the *actual* vowel sound. This situation occurs quite often in English and German, only rarely in French, somewhat in Italian, and constantly in Russian and Czech. A fine collaborator must know when to expect this delay and enjoy integrating it into the piano part. The singer is not thinking delay, merely clarity and expression; the pianist is "pronouncing" the words with her fingers; the two are together as one. I remind the reader that complete fusion with our partner is our ultimate goal.

Inflection

One can buy pronunciation guides, rules for diction can be learned, and exceptions can be memorized. When it comes to stringing words together into clauses and sentences, however, we immediately face the issue of inflection, the second, and more difficult aspect of achieving ensemble with texted music. The combination of syllables, long and short, some stressed and others almost tossed away—this is how shape is created. Without inflection, words will sound robotic, mechanical, devoid of life. There is no reference work that can inform us of how to inflect a sentence, and thus for both performers this is a more difficult challenge than simply learning how individual syllables are pronounced. Think of a beautiful necklace; each pearl may be priceless, but how the jewels are positioned will make all the difference in its worth.

Some composers strive to capture natural inflection in their vocal writing (Wolf, Ravel, Janacek, Menotti, Sondheim), and they hand us complex rhythmic recipes which seek to eliminate robotic shapelessness; others write beautiful melodies (Brahms, Tchaikovsky, Gounod, Barber) but often leave more of the task of shaping to us, the performers. In either case, inflection is a must; but the printed page cannot possibly show us everything we need to know to achieve it. Rhythmic notation is limited, but our speech patterns know no such boundaries; infinite subtleties are there to be imagined, uttered, savored, cherished. A fine singer will serve both words and music; his pianist can do no less. Remember that wonderful compliment I received about playing the words? If I had not been inflecting, I would not have earned that praise.

It must follow that if the voice part is performed with shape and the accompaniment has the same rhythm, we must replicate that shape exactly or imperfect ensemble will result. With or without linguistic fluency, as collaborators we must know the inherent shape of a group of words to be able to predict and synchronize what happens at the piano with our inflecting partner.

It is easy to understand how inflection—or, in instrumental repertoire, rubato—is too often omitted or added to the music-making far too late, as a kind of icing on the cake or special effect. We are trained from our earliest lessons to respect and revere the page, but little is said about the compromise inherent in writing music down. If the language is assigned a high enough priority, its sound and shape will enter the process early and play a far more organic role for any performer. Eventually, the pianist sees not only eighths and sixteenths, but word shapes. In instrumental repertoire, a phrase that stubbornly refuses to disclose its proper shape becomes child's play if one invents words with which to sing it.

EXAMPLE 3-1 Vaughan Williams, "Whither must I wander?"

EXAMPLE 3-2 Ives, "The greatest man"

EXAMPLE 3-2 Continued

EXAMPLE 3-3 Mahler, "Liebst du um Schönheit"

example 3-3 Continued

lie - be! Lie - be den Früh - ling, der jung ist je - des Jahr!

example 3-4 Tosti, "L'ultimo bacio"

Nes-sun lo to-glie dal-la boc-ca mi - a L'ul-ti-mo ba-cio che l'ad-dio fi-

nì; Ma se vuoi dar-gli un al-tro in com-pa-gni - a

example 3-5 Tchaikovsky, "средь шумного бала"

Средь шум-но-го ба - ла слу-чай - но в тре -во-ге мир -

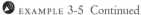 EXAMPLE 3-5 Continued

In all of these examples the performers must cope with rhythmic unison throughout, and all four languages require a generous amount of inflection. My experience as a teacher has shown me that the first response when this double challenge
exists for singer and pianist is that no one does *anything,* no one makes a move, lest
the performers risk not being perfectly synchronized. What a terrible *non-solution*
to the problem this is! The pianist must learn the shape of the text, just as the
singer does, and both performers will triumph over the limits of the printed
notation.

If a pianist wants the maximum inflection from her partner in these difficult
rhythmically unison situations, it is essential to prepare the accompaniment with
this inflection challenge in mind *before* the first rehearsal. Sometimes there is only
one natural way to say a line, whereas other texts have several possibilities. In the
latter case, the pianist should practice every conceivable option. Speaking while
playing usually leads to natural inflection almost automatically, and then singing
(by the pianist) can replace it, if she takes great care not to change the inflection
she has discovered while speaking. It is also of paramount importance that the pianist have no physical impediment; an awkward fingering or the slightest bit of
tension with a hand position change can limit flexibility ever so slightly, and this
limitation can cost us the freedom to be as natural as our partner is, a partner
without these external physical limitations of keyboard and fingers and hand posi-

tions. I have found that once a soloist feels the slightest yoke of a non-inflecting pianist limiting his very human instinct to shape the music, it is nearly impossible for him to return to that natural impulse; there will always be caution; the fear of imperfect ensemble is now implanted in the singer's mind forever. If I have doubts about how a certain unison phrase might be shaped, in rehearsal I often choose to omit notes during the first attempt together. Doing so allows me to quickly hear and understand the singer's chosen inflection without influencing it at all, or worse, permanently restricting it.

Here are some more exercises in repertoire where inflection and ensemble challenges abound:

EXAMPLE 3-6 Barber, "The daisies"

EXAMPLE 3-7 Schubert, "So lasst mich scheinen, bis ich werde"

EXAMPLE 3-8 Brahms, "Das Mädchen"

EXAMPLE 3-9 Strauss, "Allerseelen"

EXAMPLE 3-9 Continued

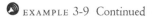 EXAMPLE 3-9 Continued

EXAMPLE 3-10 Grieg, "Jeg elsker Dig!"

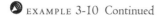

EXAMPLE 3-10 Continued

EXAMPLE 3-11 Obradors, "Con amores, la mi madre"

EXAMPLE 3-12 Rodrigo, "¿Con qué la lavaré?"

EXAMPLE 3-12 Continued

And here are some nonvocal, but highly inflected examples, too:

EXAMPLE 3-13 Schumann, Violin sonata in a minor, op. 105, ii

EXAMPLE 3-13 Continued

EXAMPLE 3-14 Chopin, Cello sonata, iii

EXAMPLE 3-15 Beethoven, Violin sonata in c minor, op. 30, #2, ii

When would no inflection be justifiable? What information would a pair of performers need to proceed in a shapeless fashion? I can think of a few cues I might encounter from a score: titles such as "Song of the Robot," "The Corpse's Serenade," or "Cement sonata, op. 5" would do the trick; another composer whose style is normally rather free might choose to put *non rubato* or *streng im Takt*

in the score as a signal to depart from his customary style; a text might describe unnatural or demented conditions such as Schumann's "Zwielicht," depicting a time of day when nothing is at it seems, or Purcell's "Mad Bess of Bedlam," with its poor heroine's wildly chaotic psyche. All of these would justify my not inflecting.

With vocal music the text is always the guide of how to proceed. How it is pronounced and how it is shaped tell us more than the most complex rhythmic notation could ever capture. We are all taught to revere the printed page, but all too rarely are we reminded that the words are part of that page, in most cases the very inspiration for the page's existence altogether! Note how much our experience of language must be brought to bear in making collaboration as complete and organic as possible.

Four

The Pianist as Designer

Having resolved issues of rhythmic ensemble, the pianist can now begin to immerse himself in some very enjoyable, more subjective challenges of collaboration. One might say, having baked the cake, it is now ready for frosting and decoration. The task of delivering the text correctly and expressively—while simultaneously making music—is not limited to the singer; without question, the pianist bears an equal measure of this responsibility. Together, the collaborators are the joint custodian of the music and the text; the pianist's role, however, extends to the implications of the text, the subtext, if you will. The voice describes something; the pianist amplifies and expands that information and experience.

Prior to even sight-reading through a new song, take the time and trouble to study the text, going so far as to read it aloud. This was the composer's initial inspiration. Note the sentence structure, and mark the vocal line of the score accordingly. Note any special features in the text, things that might ignite an actor's fantasy: maybe a twist in the agenda of the poem, a surprise, a question/answer exchange, a cast of characters perhaps. Take time to savor and appreciate the author's choice of words. There are surely synonyms available, but only these specific words were chosen . . . why? Does the sound of the word affect its appropriateness, its beauty? Your understanding and appreciation of the text will surely grow as you do this, and more important, you will be constantly constructing valuable personal expectations which the music may or may not fulfill.

The fun now begins as you incorporate the music, particularly the accompaniment, into these newly created expectations. Has the composer respected the sentence structure? Does the piano part change when ideas reverse themselves or when questions are answered? To put it disrespectfully: Has the composer made "mistakes" in creating the musical setting, mistakes which you, the performer, feel you must "fix"?

Sentence Structure and Connective Tissue

EXAMPLE 4-1 Schumann, "Im wunderschönen Monat Mai"

EXAMPLE 4-I Continued

EXAMPLE 4-I   Continued

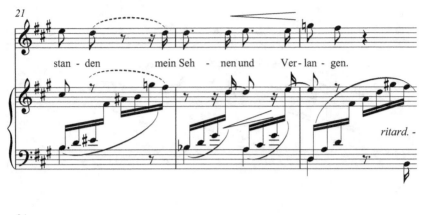

stan - den   mein Seh - nen und   Ver - lan - gen.

This ephemeral masterpiece captures nostalgic, bittersweet yearning perfectly. The birth of spring and love is described in eight lovely phrases for the voice. But we quickly note that Heine wrote only two sentences. Our text sensibilities recognize that the music needs assistance. This is what I audaciously refer to as a "mistake" by the composer. Together the two performers must convert eight into two, and since the accompaniment is continuous, it falls mainly on the pianist's shoulders to accomplish this. The keyboard must provide connective tissue to preserve the text's integrity.

The principal enemies of this connective tissue are diminuendos and ritards. If the pianist reduces the dynamics or slows while the singer is observing the rests in his part, it becomes more and more difficult and eventually impossible to preserve the complete sentence. Conversely, a slight increase in volume, perhaps a subtle accelerando can mask the singer's absence and cement the sentence fragments together. Marking the poem's needs *before* learning the piece shows the pianist his task clearly and instantly. I generally use a dotted line over the keyboard part where the voice is absent to inform myself of this connective tissue challenge.

EXAMPLE 4-2 Brahms, "Dein blaues Auge"

Schumann's colleague and close friend Brahms is guilty of the same "mistake" in this golden song. The last verbal phrase is interrupted twice, once only briefly but again with three beats of beautiful pianism. The same remedy suggested for the preceding example is called for here. Increase everything in the accompaniment while the sentence hangs unfinished, keep things bonded together, and thereby never release the audience's attention.

EXAMPLE 4-3 Schumann, "Die Lotosblume"

The composer was a highly educated person, but his knowledge clearly does not prevent him from separating the reflexive pronoun from its verb in the opening sentence. This is a no-no in the grammar of any language, and here again the pianist can be the doctor. It would be useful to have a pencil that wrote only in dotted lines, so frequently is this medicine needed in our work. As before, the pianist prevents a vacuum from existing when the singer is absent.

 EXAMPLE 4-4 Schubert, "Geheimes"

It continues to frustrate me that these great Lieder composers frequently disrespect their own native tongue. In this adorable song to a text by Goethe, Schubert greatly exacerbates the problem of an undesirable rest, first by not giving the accompaniment enough notes to truly patch the hole, and second, by asking for a fermata on the rest which ought not be there in the first place! A pianist who tapers his solo measure will make any connection truly impossible; we must strive for a minimal dimuendo. The singer can help too by not breathing during the rests, simply suspending her singing momentarily.

Quotations and Italics

Often a singer will cite someone else's words or utter something so special that it is italicized in the printed text of the poem. If the accompaniment allows the pianist to participate in this literary construction, he should try to inspire the singer's attention to this detail, and of course to mirror the structure perfectly.

EXAMPLE 4-5 Schumann, "Ich kann's nicht fassen, nicht glauben"

"It seems he said to me: 'I am forever yours.' It seems I am still dreaming. . . ." Even though German does not use the same quotation marks as we do in English, the shift in this text from third person to first and back again shows the structure clearly here. The pianist has scant material to help the singer show this shift, but one impulse is better than none. The F-sharp in measure 20, played with a different sound from the preceding chord, and timed so as *not* to elide with the singer's release of "gesprochen," can invite, even compel the singer to suggest the two voices. The chord following "dein" can do the same thing in reverse, guaranteeing the singer's return to the original color and attitude.. Timing and tone color are the designers here.

EXAMPLE 4-6 Barber, "St. Ita's Vision"

This song opens with an audacious statement: one does not often dictate terms to God, after all. But the quotation marks show us instantly that there is an interruption of two words in this bold sentence. Unlike in the Schumann example, the pianist here cannot trigger the singer's exit from the quote; that is for her alone to imagine and paint for us. But the chord following "said she" would want to be as different from the opening music as possible, not just the dynamic change asked for in the score. And what of the next chord, for we have two to play in the singer's absence? Two possibilities exist here, both equally acceptable: a V-I sort of amen to the narrator's "said she," thus making the singer return to the first-person attitude on her own, or playing the second of the two chords with a timing that propels the singer back into her quotation marks. I much prefer the latter choice, but I can be convincing either way, since the middle name of any collaborator is "flexible," after all. What is unacceptable is being unaware of the potential of the accompaniment to influence the singer. I don't want it on my tombstone that my playing allowed someone to be unimaginative or insensitive to the needs of any text.

EXAMPLE 4-7 Strauss, "Ich wollt' ein Sträusslein binden"

This is an excellent example of simultaneous character change and quotation in only one impulse from the piano. This particular character change is from an ardent human to a pleading flower—how could the pianist's solo E-flat minor chord *not* be exploited for storytelling purposes? Timing, the *una corda* pedal for a change of color, a change in the speed of attack can all help to turn this into a very special moment and guarantee that a flower's voice will follow.

"And" versus "But"

I have often felt that if singers and pianists knew only these two words in every language, considerable inroads toward expressive and specific interpretation would automatically result. For "and" there are endless substitutes that continue, extend, and prolong things; for "but" we might have a list containing the synonyms "however," "yet," "nevertheless," and so on. These are words that either tell us that nothing has changed and allow us to add innumerable items to a list, or conversely, indicate that with a single stroke all has indeed been reversed and the next thing is contrary to everything previously said. This entire chapter deals with the performer's connecting where composers have failed to do so, but this section is a more black-and-white issue. With the conjunction "and" there is no limit to the measures a composer can add, maintaining or increasing the status quo. With "but" there is no linear motion, only an abrupt stop sign, an about-face, reversing whatever has previously been in effect. It is important for the pianist, whether he has only one solo note or a full page, to recognize his function in terms of "and" or "but" and act accordingly.

EXAMPLE 4-8 Schumann, "Aufträge"

The first two stanzas of this charming strophic song feature a "but" that instantly passes the buck and blames fleeting time for the poet's failure to be properly affectionate. Here the pianist says "doch" ("but") before the singer does. If this single chord is played in tempo or in the same color as the notes before, the singer will be invited to sing "und," not "doch." A slight *luftpause*, rather like a glottal attack for the piano, can also help. It is then immediately clear to the listener—even without a translation—that the strophe's last phrase opposes all its predecessors; the black-and-white becomes audible at the piano, and no singer could ignore this effect, responding immediately in kind.

EXAMPLE 4-9 Schubert, "Der Neugierige"

Sometimes the sense of "but" or abrupt reversal is present without the actual word. The pianist invites optimism, and the lovesick miller trumpets the word "yes"; the pianist then tells us how heartbreaking the word "no" would be, and the singer responds accordingly. Our solo diminished-seventh chord must not be elided rhythmically, nor blended into the previous color, or the singer is left on his own to express his conflicting feelings. The pianist's chord is the light bulb in the singer's psyche, suddenly switched on, triggering the next words.

EXAMPLE 4-10 Wolf, "In dem Schatten meiner Locken"

Pianists need a similar technique for a question-and-answer event in a song. Three times in this sassy Spanish ditty the singer asks herself if she should wake her lover; three times she answers, "Oh no!" Whether her question is rhetorical or sincere, it still devolves on the pianist to show the exact beginning of the answer— it is two beats *before* the singer actually verbalizes it. Again, timing, dynamic, and color changes in the accompaniment win the day.

 EXAMPLE 4-11 Fauré, "Ici-bas"

The Neapolitan sixth chord on the downbeat of measure 7 represents the shift in the singer's thinking from this world to the next. This may be a modest song, and the chord may be struck quietly, but the "but" it represents is an immense one. It is preceded by a legato arpeggio, yet this trigger chord wants to be set apart in color to turn the singer's thoughts heavenward.

To illustrate the other side of the coin, here is an example of a text with no reversals; only "and" is implied here, as the singer's grateful thoughts are enumerated.

🔊 EXAMPLE 4-12 Duparc, "Chanson triste"

EXAMPLE 4-12 Continued

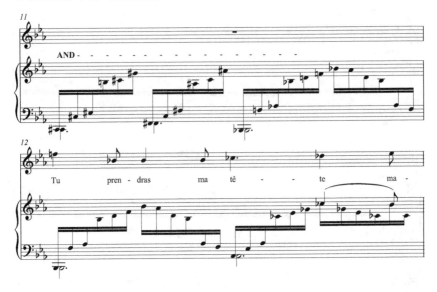

EXAMPLE 4-12 Continued

This list has many an "and" that is inferred but not uttered. With each succeeding phrase, the singer's range expands, the feelings increase, and yet between
phrases significant time exists without the singer; further separation exists between strophes with lovely two-measure solos for the piano. If the pianist is not
thinking "and" during these vocal absences, he might fail to reach the level of the
next vocal entrance, and an audible seam would be heard. I think of the accompaniment as successive locks in a canal, transporting the vessel, my singing partner, to the next level. The singer's new tessitura and dynamic have been prepared
and made inevitable by the pianist.

Casts of Characters

Nothing is more fun or more theatrical than being different characters within one
song. This obviously cannot be the singer's responsibility alone, and the pianist
must use any resource at his disposal to depict the changing personnel. Imagination, as always, is the starting point for making the necessary choices. Since most
texts with multiple characters delineate their agendas rather sharply, we are usually not restricted to hairline differences and subtleties too refined for an audience
to appreciate. In their solo moments, pianists need to ensure that they go far
enough in different directions, because they have no text to aid them as they paint
the pictures.

What are our tools? Here are just a few:

- Tempo
  Even in the strictest of styles there is still room for subtle variations of speed.
  These might imply urgency, complacency, ardor, or boredom, for example.
- Damper pedal
  There are infinite choices here. Note that "no pedal" is also a viable option.
- Una corda
  Instant color changes are available with the left foot on most instruments. Be
  sure, however, that this pedal is not being overused to control the balance, or
  the color manipulation that we need for character changes becomes obscured.
- Articulation
  Rarely will the composer's wishes be violated, but within the prescribed articu-
  lation there can be many choices from vague to very clear. Within staccato we
  have very dry or as long as possible. Within legato we have marked finger attack
  or a sensuous lack of cleanliness.
- Balance
  This refers not to the balance between voice and piano, but to the balance between the pianist's hands. Emphasizing the left hand over the right can often
  depict male vs. female, evil vs. good, old vs. young, peasant vs. aristocrat.
- Arpeggiated chords
  The speed of the arpeggio, as well as the thickness of the chord, can imply a
  variety of things, such as romance, anger, or majesty.

EXAMPLE 4-13 Schubert, "Am Feierabend"

In the middle of this fifth song from Schubert's great song-cycle, the miller introduces us to his boss, who is pleased with his performance, and in the next phrase
to his lovely daughter, who quickly retires for the evening. Unlike in many of the
previous examples, the pianist does not actually initiate these changes but immediately underlines the contrast that the singer, it is hoped, has begun just a note
or two earlier. Schubert gives the pianist the texture to easily capture the age and
authority of the father; a little too much left hand shows his sobriety and perhaps
his beard; not too smooth a repetition of the F major chord can suggest the blue-
collar nature of his work. Two quick notes from a "different" singer, and a "new"
pianist is on the scene too, now painting the femininity and grace of the young
lady. Left hand gives way to right in voicing her accompaniment; an exceptionally
clear articulation in the moving notes can show how very polite, prim, or shy she
is. All of this has happened in only eight measures!

EXAMPLE 4-14 Debussy, "Colloque sentimentale"

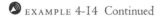

EXAMPLE 4-14 Continued

Ton cœur bat - il tou-jours à mon seul nom?   Tou-jours vois

tu mon âme en rê - ve?   Non.   Ah!_

les beaux   jours   de bon - heur   in - di - ci -

(8)- - - - - - - - -ble Où   nous joi-gnions nos bou - ches: C'est pos-si-ble

EXAMPLE 4-14 Continued

This spectral conversation features a cast of three, for the narrator's words frame the exchanges of the former lovers. The composer has given the pianist excellent tools for depicting these personnel changes, and always in advance of the singer who will doubtless follow the audible adjustments with changes of her own. We do not know the genders or ages of the ghosts here, but the optimistic versus pessimistic, or idealistic versus cynical, must be painted in only one impulse by the pianist. There is no single "correct" way to achieve this effect; the experience is too impressionistic for overly concrete choices. If we audibly differentiate the mindsets of the pair, we have done our job.

EXAMPLE 4-15 Brahms, "Vergebliches Ständchen"

EXAMPLE 4-15 Continued

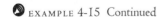 EXAMPLE 4-15   Continued

One could not find a more fertile playground for depicting characters in an accompaniment than this wonderful folk-like chestnut of Brahms. I like to make a list of pianistic choices, which would include:

He

All dynamics are generous
All rising figures crescendo;
(his ardor requires this)
Significant damper pedal
Never use una corda;
(it might seem effeminate)
Staccati are manly, heavy, full-bodied

She

All dynamics are modest
No rising figures crescendo;
(she's a good girl, after all)
Lean and clean pedaling
Una corda may be useful
(but not required)
Staccati are short, prim, leggiero

Brahms himself changes the materials for the last half of the song in mode, texture, and tempo, so the performer's job is done for him. But in the song's first two strophes, the list above is one example of a possible strategy. I would suggest that there are really four performers on stage: two singers and two pianists, all clearly stating their credentials and their agendas, and all having one hell of a good time!

FIVE

The Pianist as Director

Lighting and costumes for an opera or a play can suggest things never expressed by the actors. A film's soundtrack can manipulate our emotions before, during, or even after an event on the screen. A Wagnerian leitmotif heard in the orchestra can expand on what a character is feeling or can put the lie to what he is actually saying. In this chapter we will consider expressing that which is verbally unexpressed.

The previous chapter discussed bringing to life at the piano the things that are concretely expressed in the text: verbal structures, characters, tangible elements, textual blacks and whites. Some subjectivity was involved, but I would wager that most pianists—those intent on real collaboration in its fullest sense—would make very similar choices. In this chapter, however, we proceed to the world of implication, innuendo, inference, and suggestion. Everything is subjective here, and the score's instructions often give us little of what we need. An active and fertile imagination is the collaborator's best friend here.

Music certainly feeds the imagination, but text truly jump-starts it. For me, the text of a song is a pair of glasses through which I read the music. The importance of this issue is quickly seen when one notes that the same staccato markings are used for serenading (Brahms's "Ständchen"), sarcasm (Strauss's "Für fünfzehn Pfennige"), desire (Schubert's "Ganymed"), rage (Schumann's "Warte, warte"), and panes of glass (Wolf's "O wär dein Haus"). The same portamento markings for the piano are seen for first love (Schumann's "Seit ich ihn gesehen"), tears (Beethoven's "Wonne der Wehmuth"), and insomnia (Schumann's "Morgens steh' ich auf"). The same dynamic is requested for describing a fairy queen's nocturnal joyride (Mendelssohn's "Neue Liebe") and a group of tortured souls in Hell (Schubert's "Gruppe aus den Tartarus"), while the same tempo directions suffice for Bilitis's wandering in the snow (Debussy's "Le tombeau des Naïades") and post-coital fatigue (Duparc's "Extase"). Do I make my point? The list is endless. *There can be no musical absolutes.*

Only those musicians who deal with text can be truly certain of the appropriateness of their decisions. Is the middle movement of Schubert's *Arpeggione Sonata* sad or happy? What is the first movement of Prokofiev's sonata for cello saying, what is it feeling? Is the *Improvisation* movement from Strauss's violin sonata designed to woo, or has love already been requited? We can only hazard a guess at the composer's mood unless he has left us written instructions or a specific program. The moment text enters the picture, however, the options are narrowed, the pictures become clearer, the emotions are more specific. The words tell us almost everything we need to know.

Introductions

Songs begun by the singer alone or simultaneously with the piano constitute at most 10 percent of the entire repertoire. Most songs have piano introductions, and regardless of their length, it follows that if the singer's feelings were organized into words at the outset, the introduction would not be necessary. As we play introductions, we are describing many possible things: perhaps the singer is taking in his surroundings; perhaps the music mirrors his feelings or triggers them; perhaps he is re-experiencing a conversation or an event, plucking it from his memory and eventually articulating his reaction to it. It might be that the feelings are very strong but that verbalizing them is difficult; the appropriate words are finally formed, and the singing commences. In some songs where the piano is wholly independent—that is, *not* the singer's psyche—the pianist might represent something observed or experienced: a party, a wedding, a funeral, a river, or a will-o'-the-wisp.

EXAMPLE 5-1 Schumann, "Aus den hebräischen Gesängen"

 EXAMPLE 5-1 Continued

 EXAMPLE 5-2 Schumann, "Zwielicht"

Here are two very similar introductions crafted by the same genius in the same year. They are nearly the same length and use the identical register of the piano. They also share a slow tempo, chromaticism, and soft dynamics. That is the sum of what these two scores tell us. Now consider the texts: the first is sung by a great king, tormented and desperate for the comfort which only music can bring; the second example is sinister, downright creepy, a warning to be wary at this time of day when nothing is as it seems. How can we simply obey the musical directions without seeing them through the lenses of these poems? We have the task of making the singer's first words inevitable and necessary, as well as depicting the feelings that engender them.

The performance practice for Schumann is generally described as highly romantic, personal, and full of rubato. Exploiting this practice in the Hebrew song allows us to paint the king's pain; the chromatic introduction, played with extreme rubato, can move the singer to exclaim, "My heart is heavy." How heavy? The piano has already told us (and him) that he is inconsolable, consumed with grief.

Were the second song to be performed in a like manner, it would be musically correct, certainly Schumannesque, but it could never terrify us, for it would seem normal for this composer. The agenda here is to be as eerie as dusk, inscrutable, enigmatic, confusing. Try removing all but the slightest rubato, allowing little dynamic variation, playing as if in a trance. In the midst of a set of songs by Schumann, this approach would create something quite arresting and abnormal. Again, the poem's opening text, and indeed its whole message, is the only thing that could follow this prelude performed so unusually.

EXAMPLE 5-3 Brahms, "Von ewiger Liebe"

Let us consider two introductions here: those for strophes one and two. The music for the piano and voice is identical in both strophes; dynamics, tempo, articulations—everything is the same. But the pianist must play the *only* possible introduction for the words that follow. Verse one speaks of a world of nothingness—no sounds, no sights, not even smoke. But verse two speaks of an agitated, defensive young man escorting his beloved home. How can we expect the singer to differentiate attitudes if the four measures preceding each of her entrances are not tailor-made specifically for the text of each strophe?

The brief piano solo in question has a sweeping melodic range of a tenth, lies in a very rich part of the instrument, and, as was the case in the two previous examples, it comes from the pen of a highly romantic composer. Will a standard Brahmsian introduction to the first stanza trigger eight phrases from the singer depicting an empty nocturnal landscape? Usually when a composer uses identical material more than once, it is perfectly inspired by the first stanza, and it must be adjusted for the second. This issue will be discussed in greater detail later in this chapter when we turn to purely strophic songs. This Brahms song is an unusual case, however, for the unrest inherent in the piano solo better depicts the agitation of the *second* verse. To paint emptiness, we must proceed as was suggested earlier for Schumann's "Zwielicht," and remove all expression that could be construed as normal. For Brahms this approach is bizarre and can enhance the mysterious opening of this great ballad.

EXAMPLE 5-4 Schubert, "Suleika"

It is unusual for Schubert to introduce a song with material that is never heard again. Most often this endlessly inventive composer presents a song's credentials in its opening bars and then maintains them throughout. What can this five-bar introduction suggest? The breeze is a principal character in this song, and in the first three measures we can see first the dust, then the air itself come alive with activity. By means of these winds, our heroine communicates with her distant lover. But alas, it is not to be; in the introduction's last two bars the breeze dissipates and dies. Clearly this is not to be Suleika's day. Then suddenly, after a brief fermata, more active than before, the wind returns and now remains for pages and pages. The singer rejoices, adding grateful words to her thoughts.

Schubert is behaving very romantically in the beginning of this song, and at the piano we too must run the video in our minds of all that has just been stated. How does the breeze begin, and how will it continue? How does it die? How does Suleika feel at its reappearance? Thinking in such a pictorial and theatrical manner not only can inspire a surprised entrance from the singer, but also can transform a technically awkward introduction from an etude into a dramatic meteorological and emotional happening. My own breeze begins considerably under tempo and accelerates throughout three measures; I arpeggiate the two chords slowly, pallidly, showing Suleika's disappointment.

EXAMPLE 5-5 Schubert, "Ganymed"

This celebrated poem of Goethe's is almost too sexy for a Schubertian setting. Only the most imaginative performers can do justice to the sensuous pantheistic yearning expressed here. The materials in this introduction—diatonic to a fault, square rhythmically, laced with potentially playful staccati in the left hand—will describe neither scene nor feelings unless they are considered through the lens of the poem. I have heard this introduction sound cute, naïve, and courtly; nothing could be further from Ganymede's mind. Choosing the longest staccati possible helps enormously, as does choosing a very expressive phrasing, bordering on romantic in the right hand. Spring and lover are synonyms here, and therefore we must not be afraid to push the Schubertian envelope since the poem requires it. If the poetic sentiments are at odds with the implications of the music, we have not done our job at the piano.

EXAMPLE 5-6 Wolf, "Das verlassene Mägdlein"

Here is an example as contrary to the one above as anyone could find. Playing expressively in this four-bar introduction would make this poor girl's existence far too interesting. Nuance must be avoided here. I use my right hand for all four measures to absolutely guarantee that I don't involuntarily create variety.

EXAMPLE 5-7 Mendelssohn, "Die Liebende schreibt"

EXAMPLE 5-8 Strauss, "Die Nacht"

The introductions to another pair of songs illustrate again how almost identical material must be treated differently by any collaborator interested in delivering the poem's message. Mendelssohn's repeated pitches introduce us to an effusive, emotional young woman, someone craving reassurance, while Strauss's nocturne uses the same compositional device to express terror at the prospect of the loss of the beloved. The customary pianistic rubato serves the Mendelssohn well, but with the Strauss, six inflexible heartbeats create the ideal atmosphere. The audience is immediately alert to the fact that something is very amiss. Conventional Straussian romanticism is out of place here.

EXAMPLE 5-9 Strauss, "Das Rosenband"

This version of the Sleeping Beauty story has an interesting introduction. The first half is clearly in one key, but suddenly with the third bar, Strauss begins changing course every two beats, returning to the tonic just in time for the singer's entrance. Why does the singer *need* this harmonic wandering? Perhaps he finds himself unable to speak, given the ineffable beauty of his discovery. Perhaps this introduction depicts wandering in the forest, sensing something extraordinary ahead, but pushing aside the final visual obstacle only at the last moment before singing. Tell your own story, but these key changes must be a response to a script you are experiencing in real time as you play.

EXAMPLE 5-10 Schumann, "Heiss mich nicht reden"

The singer interrupts the pianist mid-introduction. What is the pianist saying that she will not endure? At the keyboard we must demand that Mignon speak. If we are the insistent crowd, we can provoke a thrilling first phrase from our partner.

EXAMPLE 5-11 Britten, "Now the leaves are falling fast"

EXAMPLE 5-12 Barber, "O boundless evening"

Here are two very brief preludes that share the same compositional device. Both presage music to be heard again only in the final section of each song, when the attitude of the text has changed completely. The agitation of wartime London will be silenced abruptly, and a cold, impassible mountain will end the Britten song. The introduction *is* that mountain, but it is subliminally presented three pages in advance. Similarly, Barber's gorgeous evening will be devoured and destroyed by the arrival of night, but only the pianist knows this at the outset of the song. In only three impulses we foretell this dark victory. It is debatable whether our singers really hear these introductions or whether we are informing the audience only. In order to perform these introductions properly, we must first know the end of the story, how the material will be performed when it is heard later in context. Only then do we know what this curious, seemingly unrelated material is about.

EXAMPLE 5-13 Strauss, "Morgen!"

EXAMPLE 5-13 Continued

EXAMPLE 5-14 Musto, "Litany"

The reader may think me insane to group these two songs together, but they share a very similar form. Each song is heard twice: once as a piano solo, and again with a vocal overlay. Of course one song is contemplating heavenly bliss while the other enumerates appallingly squalid earthly conditions, but in both cases the singer re-quires quite some time before words can be put to feelings. The pianist shares these feelings—how else could she play?—and if she thinks the words in the rhythms that are yet to come, the introductions acquire breadth and shape. The vocal part to come will have far more rhythmic impulses than the piano, but this busier component must have no less serenity than the long voiceless solo which precedes it. Silently pronouncing and experiencing the words while playing the piano solo guarantees repose and a perfect fit when the voice actually does enter. In other words, the pianist must account for the unexpressed impulses yet to come. Relaxed, deep breathing is also essential for the success of both of these introductions. It is unusual and a bit intimidating to be alone in the spotlight for such an extended time; the pressure is raised by the very slow tempo shared by both songs and the fact that there are but a few notes to play. One feels fairly naked playing so simply, but breathing steadies us and gives us the courage to proceed slowly. The meditative aspect of these two important songs requires these serene introductions.

EXAMPLE 5-15 Rachmaninoff, "Не пои, красавица, при мне"

EXAMPLE 5-15 Continued

Here is a rather lengthy introduction for the piano, something every collaborator looks forward to performing. In this haunting song, the singer is tormented by memories of a distant love. As long as no one sings to him, he can survive, but from the piano's first note, he is lost to painful reminiscence. Thus we are not pianists here; we are the maid herself, calling from the distant steppes. What might the words to her song be? Does her song even require words? Can she tempt him to return? She is certainly not a sophisticated or elegant singer; she is all yearning and desire, and her voice will not be silenced. I try to begin this song inaudibly, so that my audience cannot even prove that I am playing. I don't feel I am playing notes, piano keys, or rhythms. Each decoration of a principal note, be it up a half-step or a melismatic flourish, is simply a variation of longing. The extreme rubato permitted in Rachmaninoff's style is a very welcome necessity here.

Interludes

Keyboard solos that join sections are more specific than introductions because two givens are present. We know where we begin—both emotionally and plot-wise—and also where we must be when the singer re-enters. The words and feelings may be quite different when the interlude is finished, and at the piano we are the singer's psyche traveling to the new place. Again, writing a script is a necessity. I continue to use the word "inevitable," for the singer's entrance after any interlude must strike the listener as the *only* thing that could happen. Speed, volume, color, and intensity are all part of this requirement.

EXAMPLE 5-16 Schumann, "Er, der Herrlichste von allen"

This second song of Schumann's great cycle for women is composed in a rich key, E-flat major. The songs surrounding it are in closely related keys. But at the end of this poem—*not* the end of the song—we find ourselves in the land of sharps, with a three-measure interlude for the piano which will bring us home harmonically and allow our heroine to repeat the song's opening words. Poetically, we travel from "I am worth nothing" to "He's the best!" over an interlude-bridge of three bars. Thus the pianist can compose a script here with far more certainty than in introductions, since emotionally both point A and point B are known to us. I would go so far as to invent lines to say to myself in this circumstance—say aloud as I practice—lines that can end only in the breath for the singer's re-entry and her next words. How is low self-esteem put aside? And how long does it require to do so? This docking procedure must be as perfect as an inflight refueling maneuver. When the singer breathes, everything she requires for her next phrase should already be in existence. This is the very essence of the collaborator's job when playing interludes.

● EXAMPLE 5-17 Schubert, "Gretchen am Spinnrade"

This is an amazing interlude, groundbreaking when one considers that it is very early Schubert. Having lost control of her spinning, Gretchen requires three attempts to restart her wheel. If she is accomplished at this routine task, why does she fail on her first two tries? On her first try, ecstatic emotions are in the way, and the wheel does not "catch." To capture this feeling, the pianist can dare to play this first attempt too softly and/or a bit too slowly. Also a bit of rhythmic liberty allows us to slightly lengthen the rests in the right hand between attempts, giving Gretchen a moment to realize her failure to start the wheel. How does she feel at this moment? If she is frustrated, the next attempt will be stronger. But if it is stronger, why is it also unsuccessful? Perhaps she realizes just how wretched she is and her second gesture is even weaker than the first. Now how does she feel? About herself? About Faust? About tomorrow? What makes her third try succeed? I ask these questions rather than answer them, for that is the process each pianist must undergo in planning this event. We know the end result of the interlude, but there are different paths available to reach it.

 EXAMPLE 5-18 Barber, "The desire for hermitage"

The climax of this cycle of ten songs is given to the piano in this rhapsodic, expansive interlude-cadenza. The monk's vision of joyous solitude grows and grows, until words are unable to express his feelings, and the piano solo begins. At the interlude's end, eight bells summon the singer to re-enter in the modest way the song began. What is this interlude depicting? Some of my students have suggested the afterlife or perhaps the leap to heaven. I have no trouble imagining this, but my own picture is a backwards look, poised on the brink between two worlds, a survey of my whole earthly life, all that has brought me to this moment. The script here is necessarily spiritual, metaphysical, and above all, huge enough to make us play broadly and *fff* as the song's principal leitmotif is heard *marcatissimo* in the bass. This interlude must be very free, full of rhythmic and dynamic fantasy. Objectivity returns to the experience with a perfectly calculated tempo primo and diminuendo as the monastery bells usher in the singer's return to this world and its rules. The singer need not think about tempo or dynamics; he needs only to listen, breathe, and fuse with the end of the piano interlude.

EXAMPLE 5-19 Mahler, "Die zwei blauen Augen"

This fourth and final Wayfarer song is really two songs connected by this interlude. The protagonist marches sadly on, with lost love and sorrow as his only comrades. Minor and major modes are confused and confounded, the march evaporates, and only unison pitches remain for a measure. Anything could happen at this point. The pianist can treat these unisons as zero, feigning ignorance of what will follow. Mahler confuses the listener for a bar or two: duple and triple impulses coexist, and the root of the next key is postponed, depriving us of harmonic as well as emotional stability. As the pianist introduces the new accompaniment, unlike anything heard before in the entire cycle, we sense a new mindset in the traveler. The song is now bathed in a tonic pedal point; childlike melodies for both performers are clothed in soft, rich harmonies until the cycle's conclusion. Our interlude has transported the singer from obsessive trudging to a dream world, free of pain, where nothing can trouble him again. As always, the pianist calculates the perfect tempo and dynamics needed for the beginning of the next section. If the pianist has planned correctly, the actual sound of the voice is a magical surprise addition to the interlude.

Postludes

Planning the final curtain of a staged scene is as important as anything in the production. Think of the choices for the director: a dimming of the lights, an abrupt blackout, a slow curtain with the action frozen in place, an exit by all the characters, leaving the audience to contemplate what has happened—these are all possible, and they all have significantly diverse emotional effects on us. Such is the case with piano postludes to songs and arias. The words have come to an end. There may be events remaining, but more often we describe the residual feelings from the whole experience. The importance of these closing moments cannot be overemphasized. These are challenges as well as incredible gifts for the pianist. These postludes would not exist if the emotions in the song did not require them. This is a time to contemplate, a time to savor and cherish, or perhaps to rejoice, to repent, or even to learn new information the poem has left unexpressed. As you plan your performances, write the most personal and specific scripts you can.

EXAMPLE 5-20 Gounod, "L'absent"

 EXAMPLE 5-20 Continued

The singer ends his part of the experience with an expressive statement of the song's title; he hands the reins to the piano, launching the postlude. The pianist now has nearly a page of arpeggios that can suggest the expanse between the lovers, the traveling of thoughts through time and space. There is nothing dramatic here—no agitation, no harmonic, rhythmic, or dynamic interest. All is serenity, calculated by the composer, served up by the pianist. The singer seems certain of being remembered by his absent love, and the length and comfort of the postlude guarantee that he will be. Simple, confident, and rhythmically serene playing—especially when pitches repeat—will bespeak the successful rapport described here. When I think about this song, it seems never to have ended at all.

EXAMPLE 5-21 Poulenc, "Nous avons fait la nuit"

Qui   est   tou - jours   nou   -   veau

EXAMPLE 5-21 Continued

The surrealism in this cycle prevents our knowing for certain what it is expressing, but it is clear in this final song that whatever impediments to a relationship existed, they have been conquered, and the singer accepts his love for who she is. His last words, "I always see a new world through you," are almost all a pianist's imagination needs. Add to them a surprising change to C major as the postlude begins, and a pair of voices within the piano part to depict the lovers making their way through life, and the script is written. Be certain to honor the melodies in both hands equally, and give the illusion of legato in the left hand although it is not physically possible. At the very last, a reference to an earlier section, "Sillons profonds" (deep furrows where your body grows), is heard. A surprise perhaps, but as the singer has said, each day is new, and that is the fuel of this love.

● EXAMPLE 5-22 Schumann, "Waldesgespräch"

Here is an example of additional information, a final chapter in the story, if you will, written by the piano. This conversation between a chauvinistic hunter and the femme fatale of the Rhineland ends with the Lorelei's victorious statement: "You will never leave this forest!" The postlude consists not of her music as we might have expected, but of the horns that have been the hunter's signature since the song began. If a pianist respects the score's instructions carefully, this music is played quietly and legato, and this unorthodox treatment of hunting music tells us everything: his authority has been decimated, his virility compromised. Hunting music is rarely soft and never smooth; above all, it should not end on the weak third degree of the scale. Schumann, via the piano, tells us that this shell of a man will wander aimlessly forever.

I have left my two favorite postlude examples for last. There is probably not a book about song or accompanying that does not deal with these two poignant finales. I often call Schumann "Mr. Postlude" to amuse my classes, and, silly or not, the epithet is certainly appropriate. While we can certainly give Schubert credit for the creation of artsong as we know it, and award Wolf the trophy for perfect prosody in the German language, the prize for postludes goes to Schumann, hands down. Without his particular predilection for giving the closing moments to the piano, we would never know the full potential of postludes and how dramatically they can affect the whole experience of a song or even an entire cycle.

EXAMPLE 5-23 Schumann, "Nun hast du mir den ersten Schmerz getan"

EXAMPLE 5-23 Continued

Ladies first. Having begun angry and accusative, the new widow gradually drops her defenses as this song proceeds, and she finishes vulnerably, drawing into herself and her memories. Schumann then begins the piano solo with an *adagio* bar which is without doubt the most adventurous, sophisticated measure in the entire cycle of eight songs. I will postpone discussion of this unique measure just for now.

On the other side of this adagio is a complete restatement of the cycle's first song. If the pianist has been clever, she will have used the first song twenty minutes earlier not only to accompany beautifully and create the atmosphere of love at first sight, but also to acquaint herself with the mechanics and eccentricities of her particular instrument—its key resistance, its voicing, the *una corda* effect, and its color possibilities. She will certainly need that intimate acquaintance in this postlude. Dynamics are on the low side and special articulations are demanded; the control required can be achieved only with real physical understanding of the specific instrument one is playing.

The pianist must now replicate the first song in tempo, inflection (see chapter 3), nuance, and phrasing. Only singing the vocal line with text and breathing will guarantee accomplishing this. The curious articulation asked for in the first bars—disconnected but linear at the same time—poses the same problem as it will have presented in the opening of the cycle. The releases must be round, beautiful, never clipped, the rests fluid, honoring the instructions to make silences and at the same time showing the intention to be horizontal. Not an easy feat, these ambiguous directions. I have always used the motion over the barline, from eighth note to quarter note to make my decisions regarding tempo and releases; this small detail is trickiest to calculate physically. The time between phrases can be found only with real—not imagined or intellectualized—breathing from the pianist. The singer and the public must hear the entire first song as if sung again.

But an exact replica this is not! There are three points at which Schumann departs from his original. One is harmonic, the other two are rhythmic, and there is yet an articulation difference. One can imagine that the heroine intends to revisit the song exactly, but given her circumstances of unfamiliar grief, who could expect her emotions to behave perfectly? She slips and errs, as it were. Perhaps sobs catch in her throat; perhaps she is fighting a breakdown. The G-flat, the sixteenth-note B-flat, and the sixteenth rest, all new for this song, can be exploited to show her emotions and to amplify the impact of this solo. She soon regains control and completes her cycle with her accustomed poise and dignity, replicating the end of the first song precisely.

Returning now to the single adagio measure, I do not regard it as the first measure of the postlude. It is a kind of interlude unto itself, a bridge between the song and the postlude proper. As we have seen with other interludes, we know the conditions as we begin and where we must be when we end. Once one leaves the dotted note on the third beat of this adagio bar, one is committed to the tempo and expression of the next bar, and indeed to all the music that follows. Thus only five notes remain for our consideration. As the adagio unfolds, the music crescendos, and pitches are stacked up, forming the richest, most complex sonority in all of the cycle's eight songs. Clearly something very important is happening here or Schumann would not have needed to go so far afield compositionally. As each note is added in this measure, the heroine must sense the approach of the first song in her memory and its impact upon her. Is she seeking comfort in reliving the first song, or is she resisting the pain of such heartbreaking nostalgia? Answering this question will determine how a pianist performs this adagio; the crescendo and the tempo will be greatly affected by this choice. If she expects consolation in her memories, there would be little resistance to the progress within the adagio along with a warm, but not dramatic crescendo; one could imagine the word "yes" with each successive pitch. If, however, she resists opening this scrapbook lest grief overwhelm her, she would try to prohibit each successive note; "yes" is then converted to "no, no!" and this tension would create a much more dramatic crescendo and perhaps a slower, more attenuated tempo altogether. This great moment for the piano can convince us either way, but a script is absolutely required.

EXAMPLE 5-24 Schumann, "Die alten, bösen Lieder"

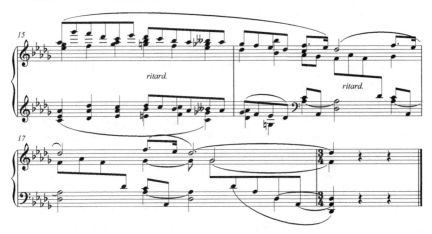

EXAMPLE 5-24 Continued

Physical death does not play a role in the ending of this cycle. There is a figurative burial, but it is an unhealthy, addictive love that is being laid to rest—no easy task. In the coffin with the poet's love is his pain. He will live on somehow, but doing so will be emotionally expensive at first. This postlude of fifteen bars is organized into three sections musically, and thus, as I have emphasized throughout this chapter, three different chapters in the script, three scenes of the video, three sets of thoughts or actions must be described.

The first six measures are a restatement of the postlude of the twelfth song of the cycle, although in a different key. Thus, as with any such reference, we can only associate the repetition with the original and assume that they stem from closely related implications. In the twelfth song it is a lovely summer day, but all is tinged with melancholy for our poet. The flowers, sisters of his love, absolve her of any responsibility for his pain. He walks on, and this postlude emerges from the flowers' music, as lovely a cantabile melody as Schumann ever wrote for the piano. Twice in two phrases, however, a disturbing, chromatic note jars us, injecting pain into beauty, the essence of this ill-fated love. Schumann uses a swell on the first of these "foreign" notes, whereas the second, although unmarked, must imprint a new harmony on the ear in only one impulse. Both of these moments require agogic accents and some additional length to succeed; the poet winces at the surprising intrusion of pain perhaps.

In the example at hand, it is very interesting that having just buried his affection in the depths of the sea as the singer finishes his part of this song, the very next thing he thinks of is his lover, as he recalls that summer day's stroll amidst the flowers. Clearly his obsession is not so easily exorcised. Unlike the closing measures of song twelve, which is extended and finds repose in a tonic chord, this restatement of the same material dissolves into an arpeggiated chord which combines tonic and dominant, a sort of question mark for the poet and the listener. "What lies ahead for me without her?" is my own subtext for this moment.

The second section is only two measures long, but more complex than the preceding phrases. The left-hand melodies inform us that the meter must change from 6/4 to 12/8, causing a new inflection in the eighth notes in the treble. Very light and transparent playing is required of the right hand, particularly in the second of these 12/8 measures, or there will be a dense, dirty clash of harmonies, given how the pedal is used here. Like the single adagio bar in the *Frauenliebe* postlude discussed earlier, these two measures form a kind of interlude-bridge between sections one and three of this solo. There the similarity ends, however, for there is an immense and fundamental difference in these two postludes: with the *Frauenliebe* solo we progress through an interlude to music whose subtext is already known to us; here, we begin with what is certain, dissolve into a two-bar interlude, at the end of which is unchartered territory with no associations. This two-measure bridge does not commit to new music necessarily; our hero could easily prove incapable of giving her up, in which case it would be easy enough for Schumann to return to the music of song twelve or even song *one!* At the end of these two bars anything could happen. These are thinking measures; they weigh love against pain; they contemplate the future and ask, "Can I really do this?" To express these questions, the pianist must use every bit of fantasy she possesses, which also helps solve the technical awkwardness of this passage. Plan the rubato according to physical needs, but disguise it as an artistic choice.

Another similarity with the Frauenliebe postlude is the dotted figure heard just before the piano commits to the next section. Permit yourself a tenuto on this E-flat, and do not fall into the next measure until the protagonist's courage is in place. This final section is a new music, far less pastel, certainly more homophonic, without ambiguous harmonies. This is the poet's new life, on his own, kicking his habit, if you will. The music *must* be unlike anything else in this solo.

If, as I am proposing, these are the poet's first "healthy" steps, then of course it is only to be expected that his first attempt to scale the heights might fail, and perhaps the second as well. (Gretchen's three attempts to restart her wheel come to mind.) With a stab of pain to mark his second failure, his resolve increases and we successfully play the whole ascending and descending phrase to its conclusion. There are occasional painful moments, particularly on the way down, but the arch is completed. He has managed to close the book on this beautiful but far too costly chapter of his life—that is, until next May invites him to reminisce again.

Strophic Songs

I cannot begin to imagine how many pure strophic songs are in my library. One thinks immediately of Gerald Moore's witty and very helpful remarks about Schubert's five-strophe song "Das Wandern," from *Die schöne Müllerin*. But be it innumerable repeated sections in an early Italian song or identical refrains in a Copland arrangement of an American folksong, this is a particular task for a collaborative pianist. In addressing this responsibility in strophic forms, we not only intensify the fusion with our partner and with the text at hand, we also can demonstrate a personal creativity which other forms would not necessarily permit or require.

Bear in mind that my philosophy about contrast in repeated sections is the same whether the composer has used a repeat sign or has written the repetition out in its entirety. Often this is the publisher's choice, not the composer's, and in the case of Schubert, one finds variation in the same song from edition to edition. How it reads is immaterial; how we perform it is the point here.

I absolutely agree with Sir Gerald that the fermata found so often at the end of the piano's introduction in strophic songs is to be observed only *ad libitum*. He postulates that this fermata was a remnant of an earlier period of music when fermatas were used to designate endings of sections, and not at all a mandatory stop before all the verses of a song.

I also feel quite strongly that one should strive to obey the composer's directions to the letter as one performs the first statement of anything that will be repeated subsequently. Just as strongly, I believe slavish obedience to those same instructions with however many ensuing reiterations is not justifiable, and in many cases, downright absurd. All of this must depend solely on the text in vocal music, and this credo applies to singer and pianist equally.

EXAMPLE 5-25 Schubert, "Die Männer sind mechant"

EXAMPLE 5-25 Continued

This very amusing tale requires the pianist to play the same solo four times, but the interpretative challenge is diminished by the theatricality of the story the singer tells. We all have a storyteller in us; some of us use text, and others—pianists—let our fingers do the talking. My approach here is, as always, to play the introduction absolutely as directed by Schubert: in a forte dynamic, with strong rhythm, bold accents in the first two measures, and the last two chords played piano, with a fermata. I cannot honestly claim to *like* the change to soft, nor the fermata, which stops the song in its tracks before the singer begins, but I feel obliged to honor Schubert's request for this.

For the second and third iterations of the piano solo, I use the text of the next strophe as my guide. By the end of each solo, I have created the conditions that are appropriate for the young lady's next chapter of her sad tale. Thus as we approach the second verse, I diminuendo in the third bar, playing much more legato. I retain the piano at the end of the solo—ignoring the fermata this time—and raise the curtain on the intimate scene to be described. I should mention too that the melodic fragments for the piano *during* the second strophe are now played stealthily, very legato, very dolce, very "nocturnally."

Verse three begins, "O mother, I must tell you, I must!" No singer would want to create these feelings on her own when her pianist is available to depict her erupting emotions. For the third solo I begin where the second strophe has ended, usually weak and dejected. I use my five bars to gradually crescendo, finishing with two forte chords—again minus the fermata, of course—which compel my partner to disclose her shocking information. The piano's interjections during this verse cannot be soft or smooth any longer; the girl is scandalized!

The postlude, my fourth time through this solo, is almost identical to the introduction. The forte is entirely appropriate now, and with my last two chords, played softly, I see the sadder-but-wiser young lady falling into her mother's arms, never to trust the opposite sex again.

When strophic songs are stories, "once upon a time" experiences, most pianists can easily devise a contrast plan and have a lot of fun doing so. However, many songs—actually the majority of the strophic repertoire—do not afford us a convenient drama that automatically does most of our scheming for us. In Brahms's eight *Zigeunerlieder*, for example, the performers repeat *everything*, with no text variation, so any and all contrast becomes an arbitrary musical decision, much the same challenge an instrumentalist confronts in any repeated section. Most of the time, however, strophic songs vary the text in repeated verses but not always with obvious or significant changes in mood. In these countless situations, a pianist must search high and low, waiting to hook contrasts on the slightest thing that might present itself. We may be painting the difference between wheat and beige, or May compared with June, or mists versus clouds, but paint we must, for not employing contrast in strophic songs is indefensible.

EXAMPLE 5-26 Schubert, "Frühlingsglaube"

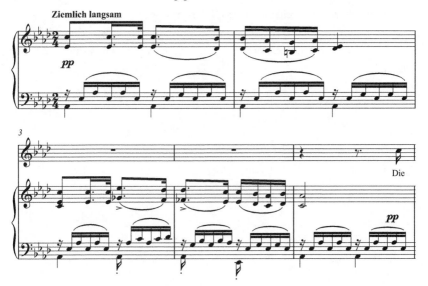

This lovely song has only two verses, but the piano solo is heard three times: as introduction, interlude, and postlude. There is also a one-measure solo for piano in the middle of each strophe. Everything is marked pianissimo by the composer, with little or no variation. Searching for something on which to hang contrast, I immediately note that the second verse begins with "The world grows lovelier with each succeeding day." These words allow me to justify playing my second solo more warmly than the introduction, finishing close to a *mf* dynamic, at which point my

partner can enter with that encouraging text. For the postlude, I attempt to re-
serve a special *pp* dynamic which bespeaks contemplation and consolation. As
softly beautiful as the introduction is, I try to "trump" it with the postlude's very
reserved dynamic and lack of too much nuance. The Sturm und Drang of life has
abated.

In the second strophe, the brief internal solo occurs with "the most distant
valley blooms" as its text. This immediately evokes the possibility of an echo for
the piano in this measure, triggering an echo from the voice in the next. In a sort
of domino-effect thought process, having chosen an echo for the second verse, I
choose the opposite effect for the identical moment in the first strophe, and all
falls neatly into place.

Again, let me say that these are arbitrary decisions, all of which could be reversed by another performer. I will, of course, strongly prefer my own choices, but
I can have no justifiable objection to other strategies, and should my partner
request something different from my original plan, I am flexible enough to create
a believable alternate. Contrast in strophic songs depends on an active, hungry,
rabid imagination. As collaborators we are as responsible for accessing and delivering this as our partners are. If I have the means to inspire, why would I not want
to do so?

Six

Kitchen Tools

We all have a kitchen drawer with the tools we use for behind-the-scenes preparations. Everything in it is necessary, and everything has its particular job to do. The guests in the dining room, enjoying the meal, might never know how each implement was used in its creation, but it would be immediately apparent if something were not up to standard. This chapter is such a collection of miscellaneous essentials. Most of the discussion here uses examples from the vocal repertoire, but much of the information would apply to instrumental collaboration as well.

Starting from Nothing (or Almost)

This can be a troublesome situation. It is far too easy to advertise discomfort and consternation, but that must never be the performers' intent. We must remove the concern and ensure that these beginnings are friendly experiences on stage and for the audience as well. For purposes of this discussion, let us assume the singer does not have the gift of perfect pitch.

There are two types of awkward beginnings to be considered. The first is either a simultaneous attack for both performers or an unaccompanied beginning for the singer after which the piano enters quite soon. If the singer feels comfortable finding the required pitch by relating it to the previous song, the pianist need not worry, nor play anything. I would suggest, however, that he always be ready to give the pitch *pppp* if the singer's strategy should fail her and an anxious head turn slightly to the right, eyes silently crying, "Help!" I have also learned—the hard way—never to take my hands off the opening notes of the accompaniment, because the singer may begin quite unexpectedly. This caution includes while turning the page—*at least one hand on the keyboard at all times!* Nothing is more horrifying than hearing a breath and realizing that one's hands are in one's lap; trust me: the distance to the keyboard never seemed greater!

If there is no introduction and the voice's beginning occurs in the first of a group of songs, two other procedures are available. The singer can get her pitch offstage from a pitchpipe or other device and make a point of remembering it while entering and taking a bow. Alternately, the pianist can walk purposefully, arrive at his instrument a bit sooner than usual, and give a soft pitch during the applause which greets the performers' entrance. Given a demonstrative, enthusiastic crowd, no one will hear or notice this. It can even be done while the pianist is still standing.

In rehearsal it is important to create a feeling of trust, confidence, and permission to take the necessary time to begin well when one is faced with this situation. Doing so requires more than just finding the correct pitch. Much is the singer's responsibility. She must construct the atmosphere, the emotion which gives birth to the opening text, and the need to sing—all without the accustomed inspiration provided by a piano introduction.

EXAMPLE 6-1 Schubert, "Heidenröslein" [adorable storytelling]

EXAMPLE 6-2 Beethoven, "Wonne der Wehmut" [profound pathos]

EXAMPLE 6-3 Hahn, "Le rossignol des lilas" [charming, friendly reminiscence]

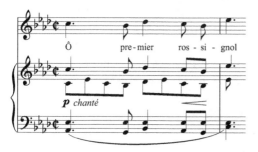

EXAMPLE 6-4 Argento, "Fancy" [whimsical improvisation]

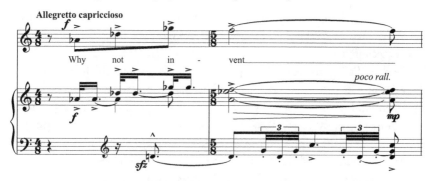

EXAMPLE 6-5 Strauss, "Schlagende Herzen" [adolescent infatuation and excitement]

In the examples above, and in hundreds more, there are obviously very diverse moods to be depicted and felt, all of which must be in place in the singer's mind and body *before* a breath can be taken. She must find the pitch, recall the opening words, and then "become" the song. She takes as long as necessary, never feeling rushed. The pianist, meanwhile, must always be ready *earlier than the singer,* so that whatever may happen, whenever it happens, the ensemble never suffers.

The other kind of tricky beginning is more subtle, more pernicious, for the score does not necessarily advertise the potential problem quite so boldly. In this situation the pianist begins and the singer enters very soon after, perhaps just a beat or even less. This problem is exacerbated when the tempo is fast, shortening the singer's preparation time to almost nothing. The pianist must imagine what this is like for the singer: she may have no idea of the new key to be introduced, nor are the pianist's first notes necessarily the pitches that she is to sing, so there is an aural puzzle to be understood and solved before she can react in song. Finally, the singer has no idea when the boom will fall, requiring her to react. And we have the temerity to expect a comfortable, expressive entrance, given all this?

I have heard pianists give the opening pitch in this situation, but I have never considered it quite legal to do so myself. After all, there is music before the singer begins. I never allow myself this easier solution, although I would accede to a singer's request to do this. Before agreeing, however, I would try some of the following techniques:

Remove the "when" part of the problem. This is accomplished easily enough. If the pianist breathes audibly as he lifts his hands to play, the singer will never be surprised. I am often asked by a slightly horrified pianist, "What if the audience hears this breath?" and I marvel at people who think it incumbent on performers to be silent or non-human. Even if the singer does not need to hear me breathe, it would be difficult for me to begin without an inhalation for my own purposes in any case, and here it is doubly necessary. In this potentially awkward starting situation, it is imperative for the singer to hear the pianist's physical preparation, and in the appropriate tempo and mood. Thus one unknown is removed. If the vocal entrance is extremely soon after the pianist's first notes, it is probably advisable for the singer to breathe before her partner, triggering this multistep process:

1. Singer breathes and is now fully ready with air, attitude, and text.
2. Pianist breathes audibly and begins to play.
3. Singer listens and reacts comfortably and gracefully with her entrance.

I list these as three steps, but when they are done fluidly and comfortably, this beginning becomes a single smooth event.

Having settled *when* to sing, what remains is the *pitch* part of the problem: finding the correct opening notes. The singer must organize the all too brief material she hears into a harmonic context, and doing this takes a moment, even for the best of musicians. My solution is to begin the piece a bit under tempo and accelerate. There are very few songs that cannot tolerate this treatment. When the real tempo is achieved depends on many factors: the style, the emotion, the vocal and aural difficulties encountered. Let us always insist on being practical. No singer will begin well with only mental hurdles to be jumped, all in the name of accuracy. What is accuracy anyway? Does it not require expression? Confidence? For me, good musicianship must include being musical.

Here are several examples of this second type of nasty beginning:

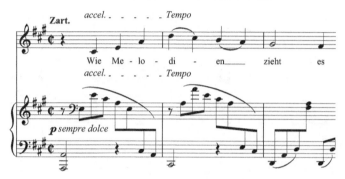

EXAMPLE 6-6 Brahms, "Wie Melodien zieht es mir"

Allow the downbeat to communicate the key to the singer. The right hand can easily enter a trifle late, justified by the rubato and romanticism inherent in Brahms's style. One can use the entire first measure to gently accelerate to tempo. This song is only about intangible things, so why be rigid at the start, advertising the wrong product *and* scaring our partner?

EXAMPLE 6-7 Brahms, "Meine Liebe ist grün"

This is a similar example, but in a much faster song. The first beats are stretched, and the rest of the bar accelerates. Tempo is reached only at the beginning of bar two. The sumptuous sonority of the accompaniment disguises this very practical treatment.

EXAMPLE 6-8 Wolf, "In dem Schatten meiner Locken"

The pianist's downbeat could really be the end of an imaginary preceding bar; this will soon prove to be the case with this motive for all of this song. Pause ever so slightly after the downbeat, and make sure your singer is ready before you proceed into beat two. Because of the dancelike quality of this accompaniment, accelerando is ill-advised here. The tiny pause after the first beat works wonderfully in its stead; it is nearly undetectable and instantly creates the Spanish flavor. More important, it will not leave the singer behind at the starting gate.

EXAMPLE 6-9 Berlioz, "Sur les lagunes"

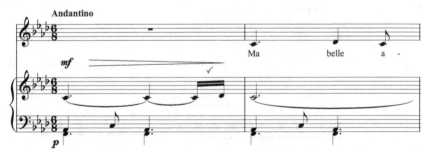

It would have been so much more practical for the composer to have given us *two* bars of rowing before the singer enters, but alas, that is not the case. If a pianist does not want to stop on the sixteenth note in bar one, he should be absolutely certain that the singer has inhaled and is already forming an "m" before proceeding out of the measure.

EXAMPLE 6-10 Satie, "Daphénéo"

This is not a difficult pitch to find, given that the preceding song in this brief tryptich ends only a half-step above. Even so, there remains an immense color change, a song with two very different characters to be created, and only two eighth-notes to initiate all this. I put a slight tenuto on the downbeat. If I'm confident my singer is ready, I add the second note in tempo and we proceed.

EXAMPLE 6-11 Poulenc, "Reine des mouettes"

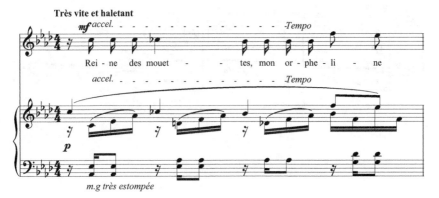

This is surely one of the worst cases in anyone's list of starting issues. Only a single sixteenth note in a *molto allegro* tempo to hear, and the singer must then organize the key, flip an "r", enunciate the nasty combination of sounds in "des mouettes," and *seem* to begin whimsically—what was Poulenc thinking? Even though his performance practice stipulates no rubato, this tricky beginning is simply not possible without it. It is imperceptible to the audience if the tempo is actually reached on beat three of the first bar.

EXAMPLE 6-12 Argento, "Spring"

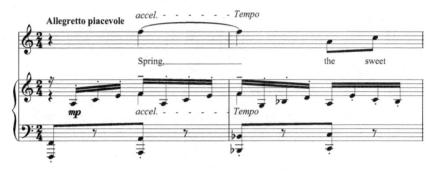

EXAMPLE 6-13 Argento, "Sleep"

EXAMPLE 6-14 Argento, "Hymn"

Three times in one song-cycle we must deal with this issue of starting beautifully yet practically. In "Spring" the right hand can enter a bit late and accelerate throughout the first bar to tempo in the next, rather similar to the treatment I suggested for the two Brahms examples above. Note that the singer here must put three consonant sounds *before* the vowel, and we have already learned that the vowel *is* the beat, *is* the music. With "Sleep" a slow arpeggio with the melodic pitch (F) played last does the job; it gives the singer just an extra second to organize what she is hearing. Finally, in "Hymn" the singer creates the tempo herself. The pianist breathes audibly as always, but since the tempo is moderate and the right hand is in unison with the voice, this beginning is the least problematic of the three.

Remember that in all of these cases, with both types of awkward beginnings, *any feeling of difficulty or worry must absolutely be avoided,* and certainly never communicated to the audience. The earlier this comfort is introduced into rehearsals with one of the techniques described above, the more guaranteed the friendly final product.

The Unreachable

The title of this section does not refer to the Man of La Mancha's dream; nor is it about an event in the accompaniment for which the pianist is specifically requested to arpeggiate or break a chord. Except for the lucky ones whose reach extends much beyond average, the rest of us, with human-sized hands, will always face quandaries about playing chords and clusters that we cannot strike as one impulse despite the composer's desire that we do so.

The first thing to be considered is sheer practicality. Often a very quick tempo will not allow for breaking a chord and playing accurately, especially if the preceding impulse is itself awkward, distant, or tense. Issues of clarity and practical pedaling must also be weighed when one is making these decisions.

If accuracy and clarity issues have been satisfied, we can proceed to more engaging questions. Consider the emotional implications of arpeggios versus broken chords. If arpeggiation is chosen, one must also consider the speed of the roll and whether it crescendos as it proceeds. If one opts to break something unreachable, one must decide how it is to be divided; is its foundation a single note, a fifth, an octave?

⁂

EXAMPLE 6-15 Strauss, "Allerseelen"

In the last stanza there are two moments which many of us cannot reach: "ist ja den *Toten* frei" and the first statement of "*wie* einst im Mai." In the former, there is virtually no time from the previous note, so comfort and accuracy will be the basis of our decision to roll or break. The fortissimo chord on "wie," however, following a broad silent beat as it does, allows us both choices. For me, an arpeggio bespeaks love and heartbreak whereas a broken chord, with a single bass note played as a grace note before the beat, implies desperation and very raw emotion at the loss of the beloved. These implications are very personal and thus different for each of us. The important thing is to realize that different implications exist and that, as collaborators, we are charged with these choices that affect our partners and our listeners in ways both conscious and subliminal.

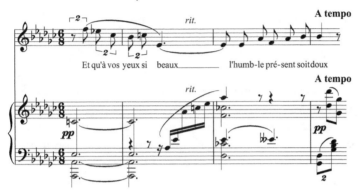

EXAMPLE 6-16 Debussy, "Green"

Between two halves of a sentence, "Et qu'à vos yeux si beaux" and "l'humble present soit doux," there exists a written-out arpeggio and a hard-to-reach chord which follows immediately. Some singers need or choose to breathe after "beaux," while others do this in a single phrase. At the piano, arpeggiating takes more time; this will aid and abet the singer's decision to breathe. If, however, the vocal goal is all four bars without breathing, a quickly broken chord is surely more accommodating to the singer's preference.

EXAMPLE 6-17 Ives, "The cage"

There are many extended chords for both hands in this single page of music. The warmth, love, humanity, or pathos that an arpeggiated chord can imply would all be entirely inappropriate here. This poor creature leads the most tedious of lives; only unfeeling broken chords can depict such a useless existence.

Silence—Golden and Not

Silence is unquestionably the most dramatic tool a performer possesses. It is available for theatrical moments, for setting something apart or highlighting it, for exploiting a musical or textual event just finished or the next to come. I am referring here to those silences that may be inserted by the pianist during a song—internal silences, if you will, not the silences on either side of a piece, which I will discuss elsewhere. Nor are these the obligatory silences notated on the page as part of the composer's instructions; these silences are consciously chosen by the performers.

Precisely because it is such an unusual effect, we must be certain that silence is not used too frequently. As with anything special, the more often it is used, the less currency it has. We appreciate a single cymbal crash at the climax of an orchestral piece, but we hardly hear the constant use of the same instrument in the march of a military band. Silence must be protected and never allowed to become the norm or the expected. Used judiciously and infrequently, it will retain its full potential.

EXAMPLE 6-18 Schumann, "Seit ich ihn gesehen"

EXAMPLE 6-18 Continued

Trau - me schwebt sein Bild____ mir vor,____

Sometimes, in the name of "fine" accompanying, one hears the pianist inserting silence whenever the two performers have rhythmic unisons and the singer breathes. This unfortunate decision is probably intended to be helpful and collaborative, but in fact it peppers the performance with so many silences that this marvelous effect is drained of all its potential. In addition it highlights each and every absence of the singer or woodwind player. In this example, where silence is used indiscriminately, no fewer than three silences in four bars would be heard. The performers are synchronized, but not much else could be lauded. Performing correctly, the pianist sustains the chord while the singer breathes, and both proceed together when the singer reenters. No silence is ever heard from both performers simultaneously in this song.

Compare what I am advocating here to a chorale in a Bach passion or the end of a phrase in any woodwind quintet. In those cases, breaths and silences are synonymous, physical necessities. That must not be the case with music with piano accompaniment except by design.

EXAMPLE 6-19 Vaughan Williams, "Bright is the ring of words"

Moderato risoluto

Bright is the ring of words - When the right man rings them,

EXAMPLE 6-19 Continued

Here is another example, rife with numerous undesirable silences which would be created if the pianist always equated time to breathe with simultaneous, mutual, and complete silence. As before, the pianist glues the singer's phrases together by sustaining the chord at the moment of the singer's absence, allowing him ample time to breathe but not creating holes in the fabric unless a special effect is desired. Remember too that a special effect, by its very definition, cannot occur multiple times.

So when do we employ this "special" mutual silence? Remember, this is the performers' choice. I use the plural advisedly, for although the pianist executes the silence, the vocal part is nonetheless affected too. A request to insert silence may originate with the singer, or it may in fact be the brainchild of the pianist, with the singer being conscious only of the magic it imparts. If this effect is well chosen and organically integrated into the piece's agenda and atmosphere, it will seem the only artistic choice for that moment.

EXAMPLE 6-20 Mahler, "Liebst du um Schönheit"

Rückert's admonition to love for the right reason is structured poetically with three times "don't" and one time "by all means, do!" Throughout this song the performers are in melodic and rhythmic unison. At the end of the third section, the singer breathes quite naturally for the new thought, the change of direction, and, as is always the case, creates a silence during the breath. If the pianist inserts the same pause, then mutual total silence occurs; this will doubtless trigger a new color from the voice, and the effect on the strophe's beginning can be quite marvelous. The audience thus hears complete silence for the first and only time. The listener may not be conscious that it is silence which creates the magic, but that magic is palpable regardless. There are numerous other opportunities for this same effect in this song; they are all musical and possible, but I would absolutely avoid them. The uniqueness of this single silence is thus protected and isolated, its effectiveness magnified.

EXAMPLE 6-21   Schubert, "So lasst mich scheinen, bis ich werde"

 EXAMPLE 6-21 Continued

Here is a similar example in Mignon's plea, but with a longer text and therefore more musical sections. Still, a clear division between Mignon's vision of her heavenly future and her single reference to her wretched earthly history occurs at the words "Zwar lebt' ich." The tiniest eyelash of silence in the piano part sets apart the next words, deeply and painfully felt, from all the ecstatic preceding lines. This moment is particularly welcome in this song, for Schubert has not changed the music very significantly, given this immense reversal in the poem. Anything we can do at the piano to inspire our singer to be more specific, to use contrasting colors, and to illustrate the organization of Mignon's thoughts for the audience is surely worth the trouble.

 EXAMPLE 6-22 Duparc, "Le manoir de Rosemonde"

EXAMPLE 6-22 Continued

Here is an interesting example of choosing *not* to insert a silence, although the temptation is certainly great. In the final section of this highly dramatic song there is a moment of melodic and rhythmic unison for the performers ("bien loin, bien loin"). The hero—or should I say antihero?— confesses the absolute failure of his life. "I destroyed myself far away, far away . . . without finding Rosemonde's mansion." Creating a mutual silence at the repeat of the words "far away" would be a marvelously theatrical effect. But if one looks just one phrase further down the road, one sees an obligatory rest for both singer and pianist. We can conclude therefore that Duparc felt that the tragic futility was felt more deeply at the words "sans découvrir" ("without discovering") than at the tempting word repetition two bars earlier. We give up one dramatic moment to achieve another. Two *coups de théatre* in two adjacent phrases would equal *pas de coups* altogether.

EXAMPLE 6-23 Hundley, "Come ready and see me"

In this American favorite, the form Hundley employs is A-A'. Unlike a strophic song where words change in successive verses, this poem is heard twice through entirely with the sole exception of its first lines. Interpretatively, this form poses inherent problems for the performers, for why would one say everything again, accompanied almost identically? The emotional need to repeat must be constructed; the subtext must reign in the repetition, not the text. One looks for any nook or cranny of potential contrast that can be imposed on the second A section to justify its existence. It is possible—not required, mind you!—to enlarge the subtext for the words "under the bluest sky," to increase the desperate urgency of the singer's plea. If one chooses to read the line in this way, a simultaneous silence from both performers can be justified and can provide a very audible contrast to the same moment in the first strophe.

EXAMPLE 6-24 Vaughan Williams, "Bright is the ring of words"

I used this example earlier to caution against making mutual silence in any way routine. Here, however, I cite it again for its ending, where the experience might be enhanced by the use of this effect of mutual silence but a single time. For me, this song is about the possibility of immortality, about lovers using a poet's words to connect with one another and with all couples, past and future. The girl's memories are crucial here; without them the boy's songs would be forgotten, sung in vain. Thus the song's last sentence, delivered expressively, would read: "The lover lingers and sings . . . and the maid remembers." Inserting a silence in the accompaniment at the end of the arpeggio, after the singer has enjoyed the final consonants in the word "sings," lends something very poignant to the maiden's role here. It is she who completes the circuit and guarantees immortality. Note how powerful this small silence can become in this context.

EXAMPLE 6-25 Vaughan Williams, "Linden Lea"

We are concerned here with the last vocal phrases in the song.

> I be free to go abroad,
> Or take again my homeward road
> To where for me the apple tree
> Do lean down low in Linden Lea.

In this third stanza the accompaniment is in rhythmic unison with the singer, so the opportunities for mutual silences abound. If one sought a very personal, sentimental reading, one with a tear in its eye, it would be justifiable to use silence twice here. This section begins boldly, emphasizing virility, freedom, and wanderlust, but a mutual breath for both performers after "abroad" ushers in an immense change to tenderness, vulnerability, and the sweetness of going home. A second silence before "in Linden lea"—words we have heard in two previous stanzas without a breath or any exaggerated sentiment—certifies this meadow as the dearest place in all the world, and it shows how potent a subtext—and a silence—can be. Remember that employing two silences so close to each other constitutes the most *extreme* of exceptions!

A final word about all these wonderful silences: whether they are chosen to create contrast, to wake people up, to paint dramatic events, or to make the listener feel something special, they will always enlarge the meaning of whatever follows. Subtext is unusually close to the surface, and as a consequence these calculated silences will feel completely sincere and emotionally justified.

Imitation in Its Sincerest Form

When a pianist imitates what has just been sung or played, the audience usually hears a restatement of the same words and notes, identically pronounced and inflected, and of course, describing the same feelings. Perhaps the dynamic will vary—softer to suggest physical distance or louder for emphasis—but all else will remain a perfect carbon copy of the original.

Bear in mind, however, that carefully replicating the shape and timing of the phrase when imitating is not enough. If a pianist carelessly elides his solo to the end of his partner's initial statement, the result is simply a longer event, and there is no imitation. *We do not say things twice without punctuation.* "I love you I love you" might be an amusing line from e.e. cummings or Gertrude Stein, but it is certainly not the same as "I love you. I love you." We must simulate the time that our partner would take to breathe and repeat the phrase herself.

EXAMPLE 6-26 Schumann, "Seit ich ihn gesehen"

hel-ler, hel-ler nur   em-por.

EXAMPLE 6-27 Schubert, "Der greise Kopf"

Der Reif hat ei - nen   wei - ßen Schein mir   ü – bers Haar ge - streuet;

da glaubt' ich schon ein Greis zu sein   und

hab   mich sehr ge -   freu - et.

EXAMPLE 6-28 Beethoven, "Wo die Berge so blau"

EXAMPLE 6-29 Barber, "Promiscuity"

● EXAMPLE 6-29 Continued

These four songs all feature imitation multiple times. We have already discussed inflecting at the piano, recognizing the limitations of rhythmic notation, and allowing the text to dictate the shapes of phrases, so we can assume that the relative lengths of the notes in these imitations will match the originals exactly. It is *when* the imitation begins that concerns us here.

The only way to know how much time is required between the original and the imitation is to sing both—that is the physical sensation we are attempting to describe, *not* two people saying something, but *one* person saying something *twice.* The timing between phrases will be affected by tempo and the difficulty of the first statement of the twin phrases.

In the examples by Schumann and Schubert, the phrases to be repeated are long and technically demanding. In addition, these are both very emotional songs. Therefore the recovery time after the first phrase is significant; sing them both and let your body teach you the correct moment to begin the imitation. (I realize that in the Schubert example the imitation is slightly changed in pitch and ornamented, but that fact in no way changes the timing we are discussing here.)

In the example from the Beethoven song cycle, the phrases are only four notes long—mere fragments of a sentence—and the tempo is moderate, so the simulated breathing time between phrases can be miniscule. With Barber's "Promiscuity" too, very little additional time would be required to imitate convincingly, but that is *not* to say that *no* time whatsoever is necessary. Remember that the breathing clock begins ticking *only* when the singer finishes the last note before the pianist's reiteration of the phrase.

In all instances of imitation, do not confuse the required time between phrases with the option of inserting silence between them. The former is absolutely necessary while the latter is always a personal choice; if used too often, silences will undermine their own effectiveness, as we have already seen multiple times in this very chapter. These are two totally different and independent choices with very different results.

Double or Nothing

There are two subjects to be discussed under this heading: the accompaniment doubling the soloist's line and the use of unison for special coloring and dramatic effect.

I fear that with the first of these two headings, I may be all alone in my convictions. I have heard so many of my colleagues express a philosophy contrary to mine, so be advised that what follows is probably the minority opinion. The quandary is: should the pianist show or even exploit the doubling of the vocal or instrumental line, or should he highlight a different voice in the keyboard part to avoid too much emphasis on the same tune?

If my vocal or instrumental partner were removed, leaving me with a piano solo, I doubt there would be much controversy about which line to make predominant. One might enjoy other voices to add interest and complexity, but rarely would the melody be ignored altogether. If the tune were harmonized closely—one thinks of Brahms's thirds or sixths, for example—we might plump up the duet line with its alto or tenor sibling to add richness, but never to the exclusion of the principal melody. I would never advocate changing any of this philosophy simply because one is collaborating with another. The voicing I would choose in a solo remains in place as I collaborate.

I cannot help noticing too that the same composer will now decide to double the soloist's melody in the piano, and on another occasion decide against doing so. This decision does not seem to depend on any consistent condition; tempo, register, dynamic, and attitude seem to play no role. I wonder then why we should avoid underlining the presence of the doubling. We can choose to see this issue both ways: the doubling makes the sound of the duo special, *or*, having the soloist in relief, undoubled, makes that line special. In my view, both viewpoints require exploiting the doubling—or at least, not hiding it—whenever it is present.

I can also think of some wonderful moments in operatic repertoire where, after a time without it, doubling suddenly appears. Mimì's "Ma quando vien lo sgelo" in her first act aria or Cherubino's "Non so ch'il tiene, non so cos'è" in his love song sung for the Countess both come to mind. These are special moments, in part because the accompaniment fuses *with* the singer melodically, and we welcome this new orchestration. Even the untrained listener appreciates the difference, although he might not know what makes the music suddenly more sumptuous.

Conductors would not hide this change of orchestration, and most would seek to take advantage of it. Why should music for piano accompaniment be treated any differently?

EXAMPLE 6-30 Schubert, "Der Wegweiser"

EXAMPLE 6-31 Schubert, "Lied der Mignon"

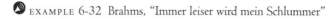

EXAMPLE 6-32 Brahms, "Immer leiser wird mein Schlummer"

EXAMPLE 6-33 Brahms, "Die Mainacht"

EXAMPLE 6-34 Schumann, "Wehmut"

EXAMPLE 6-35 Schumann, "Mondnacht"

In this list of six songs, each composer's pair features one song with vocal doubling and one without. The general musical style is the same for both pieces in each pair, as is the performance practice. The Schumann examples are even from the same cycle. I feel the two songs in each pair should not be made to sound alike. Show off the vocal doubling—it is the composer's specific orchestration choice; voice the piano part as if it were a solo.

There are innumerable examples of this type of doubling which can be found in instrumental repertoire as well:

EXAMPLE 6-36 Beethoven, Violin sonata in a minor, op. 47, ii

EXAMPLE 6-37 Brahms, Violin sonata in d minor, op. 108, ii

The middle movement of Beethoven's Kreutzer sonata features this doubling of violin and piano in the theme itself and again for the variation in the minor mode. It is withheld for all the rest of this long movement, and thus I would elect to emphasize it on these two occasions. Brahms's principal theme is heard three times, but doubled only once, at its second appearance. Since the violin is an octave above the right hand of the piano, balance is not at all a problem; I like to think of these measures as scored for violin I and II, both playing their expressive best.

Assuming my remarks here have had some success in converting pianists to enjoying doubling, there are two situations which would make me reconsider and strive to camouflage any doubling. First, whether it be vocal or instrumental, if my partner is unable to perform a doubled passage in perfect tune with the piano, *particularly* if the doubled notes are in the same octave, I would never want to bring the audience's attention to the intonation discrepancy. Second, if perfect synchronized ensemble has proven elusive or inconsistent, even after significant rehearsal, I would avoid the risk of advertising this difficulty in performance and play the doubled passage in question very discreetly.

The other half of this subject of doubling fortunately does not seem to inspire controversy or conflicting opinions, at least not to my knowledge. This concerns doubled passages where the composer's agenda is unison, unharmonized pitch for both instruments. This is an unusual sound, often used for eerie, bleak or spectral moments, and both performers should make sure these moments, no matter how brief, strike the ear as special events. This can happen only if the pianist exploits the unison doubling. Regardless of the dynamics, the pianist will want to use an incisive, very focused touch for these passages, and whether his partner be a singer or an instrumentalist, she too should choose minimal or no vibrato and a lean sound that has little or no sensuous component. Thus the two instruments can really succeed to sound as one, doubled or tripled at the unison.

EXAMPLE 6-38 Schubert, "Ihr Bild"

The thrust of this song is the surprise of an inanimate portrait suddenly coming to life after only a phrase or two. Schubert juxtaposes an eerie unison beginning with a spontaneously harmonized accompaniment to display the two extremes. Using *una corda* and almost no damper pedal for the opening section, along with very clean articulation, makes the metamorphosis particularly effective.

EXAMPLE 6-39 Schumann, Romance for oboe and piano, op. 94, #3

This final installment in a group of three pieces for oboe and piano is in the key of a minor, as lonely and melancholy a key as can be found. The two instruments are in perfect unison, doubled at the octave, for both the initial section and its reprise. After each mournful phrase, the piano contributes a harmonized comment of two simple chords. The communal unison sound must haunt the listener. This movement, incidentally, is also a nightmare for rhythmic ensemble. The unison coloring I recommend here is actually the easier part of the pianist's job.

EXAMPLE 6-40 Brahms, "Feldeinsamkeit"

EXAMPLE 6-41 Brahms, "Ich wandte mich"

In this pair of songs we find very brief unison episodes, each a foil for the rich, harmonized texture immediately surrounding it. Note how the poetic phrases which inspired Brahms to use unison are so closely related in atmosphere: "It seems as though I had died long ago" and "And he who does not exist [is better off]." Again, a mutual *lack* of color *is* the very color we select to best describe these conditions.

Finishing Touches

Music, like any art form, is rich in clichés. Our venerated composers have created traditional associations, perhaps without even realizing it, or perhaps a cliché already in existence is used quite consciously. As collaborators, our ability to serve the poem is often aided by these customary gestures, and we should not disdain or avoid them simply because they have become stereotypes. At the same time, however, we must make certain that the usual association fits the specific situation.

For example, when we hear high staccati, we probably think playfulness when in fact it might be Mozart's evil Queen seeking vengeance. Tradition tells us that minor modes are supposed to be sad and major ones happy, but then what do we make of the end of Schubert's "Doppelgänger" or "Die Liebe hat gelogen," songs that utterly reverse these customary associations? Sometimes the use of a traditional musical gesture is inappropriate for the text in question or the experience as a whole. I find this particularly true with the tonic chord—or worse yet, a series of tonic chords at the end of a piece.

EXAMPLE 6-42 Brahms, "Vier ernste Gesänge," ii, iii, iv

Here is the most traditional use of final tonic chords. These biblical texts are huge statements about life and death, vocal symphonic movements, and each wants an appropriate "Amen!" as it comes to a contemplative, majestic close. There is no questioning what the singer tells us here; it comes from on high, after all. The respect we pay to such exalted philosophy makes these traditional extended tonic endings entirely fitting.

The preceding examples and thousands more use the tonic repetitions to seal their case, stamp their message "Approved," and draw the curtain on the experience with authority, be it loud or soft. Occasionally, we might even add a small *luftpause* before the last of these chords to heighten the effect, to lend even more importance to the final gavel's descent. We would not want this breath to become predictable or routine, but, as we have seen, silence, used sparingly, is a most useful and theatrical tool for the pianist.

Having had an example of the most traditional use of this final gesture in the piano, we can now better observe when its use is out of place.

EXAMPLE 6-43 Vaughan Williams, "The roadside fire"

Call this ending another "mistake" of the composer, if you will. This song is an invitation. "Will you come and live with me?" it asks, and it offers a detailed view of a joyous future together—*if* your answer is yes. Although the text does not end with a question, the singer clearly throws the ball into the girl's court. These final tonic chords therefore must not finish the experience. In fact, calling them final is in itself a misnomer. The subtext here is "How about it? Shall we?" and the pianist should think of the chords as upward gestures, question marks, certainly not final periods. Any sense of ritard or closure must be avoided if the pianist is truly sharing the singer's mindset; a subtle accelerando through the chords to the final double bar would also not be unwarranted. "To be continued," says the pianist; there is no "Amen" here.

EXAMPLE 6-44 Schubert, "Das Fischermädchen"

This is a first cousin to the previous example—another song of wooing, a little less specific about the future, but a kind of invitation nonetheless. This postlude can be nuanced, but it should maintain the level of clever sophistication heard throughout the song. To finalize the last four tonic chords in a stereotypical manner would lack the elegance and wit that the gentleman has displayed when singing. If you must have a closing nuance, choose an earlier, less predictable place than the final chord, and leave the maiden astonished and speechless.

EXAMPLE 6-45 Wolf, "Auf einer Wanderung"

In this postlude the wanderer, moved by his excursion in the countryside, stops, turns, and considers the distant golden city one last time, and then. . . . no fewer than nine tonic chords! Surely the two measures Wolf has marked *ausdrücksvoll* contain the last real nuance in the song; after this beautiful phrase, anything else would seem superfluous. After all, it's time for our happy traveler to get on home.

EXAMPLE 6-46 Fauré, "J'allais par des chemins perfides"

All the previous examples have featured tonic chords around or below middle C. This example features the high register of the piano, but the principle remains the same: The words and agenda of the text must be our sole guide in planning our performance of these final chords, and as we have seen, they may be the last measures of the song, but they are not always final with regard to their emotional function. This song has traveled from rocky paths to conjugal bliss; love has conquered all and united us in joy. How do we paint those sentiments in three chords? Any ritard would be entirely out of place. Open the door on this relationship; don't close it! For tools use the brightness of Fauré's choice of key, the register of the piano, a sharp diamond-like attack, and a quick arpeggio.

A brief word about harmony and its effect on nuance is appropriate here. You may have noticed a consistent thread: The last harmonic event in these songs is not found in their final measures. I doubt that it is universally true, but I suspect that most of the time the appropriate place for a final nuance from the pianist would be the last *real* event in a song, and that would normally involve a harmonic change. This is certainly true for all of the examples above. Consider these two Schubert songs, both youthful, bold, animated experiences:

EXAMPLE 6-47 Schubert, "Wohin?"

EXAMPLE 6-48 Schubert, "Fischerweise"

In the first example, *if* a final nuance is to be made (and that's a big "if"), I would choose the singer's last two words as the ideal place for it, *not* the end of the post-lude three bars later. The accompaniment changes from dominant to tonic for the last time as the singer finishes. I would then suggest playing absolutely in tempo, forgoing any further ritard. Not only does this approach emphasize the poem's conclusion, it also illuminates the last harmonic change and thus the last authentic event of the song. Since the piano takes the role of the brook here, it also allows the water to maintain its flow. It is still babbling, even if we can no longer hear it.

In "Fischerweise," another festive water song, we have quite a different situation. Here the last harmonic *as well as* melodic event is found in the postlude's final two notes. If nuance is desired to close this song, it must be at the final cadence, either with a tasteful, slight ritard, or perhaps a cute, witty *luftpause* before the last chord. As an experiment, add two additional bars of tonic quarter- and eighth-notes to make these two Schubert songs share identical endings. You will note how the nuances are in the same places. Remove the added measures, and the final nuance of "Fischerweise" remains where it was originally. A book could be filled with examples illustrating this compositional tendency on the part of song composers. As performers we must be aware of this and plan our final expressive moments accordingly.

Here is a list of some well-known songs in which the last "event" is not at the end. The consistency here is readily apparent:

EXAMPLE 6-49 Schubert, "Halt!"

EXAMPLE 6-50 Schumann, "Widmung"

EXAMPLE 6-51 Brahms, ""Der Tod, das ist die kühle Nacht

EXAMPLE 6-52 Strauss, "Ständchen" [Strauss's pedal indications would seem to confirm my philosophy.]

EXAMPLE 6-53 Fauré, "Après un rêve"

EXAMPLE 6-54 Britten, "Seascape" [NB: Here the added sixth to the tonic changes nothing.]

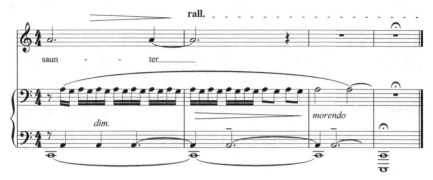

From the same composers, here is a list of the entirely opposite situation; in all of these cases the last event *is* at the very close:

EXAMPLE 6-55 Schubert, "Des Baches Wiegenlied"

EXAMPLE 6-56 Schumann, "Die Lotosblume"

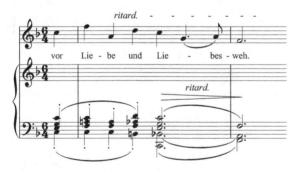

EXAMPLE 6-57 Brahms, "Vergebliches Ständchen"

EXAMPLE 6-58 Strauss, "Morgen!"

EXAMPLE 6-59 Fauré, "Automne"

EXAMPLE 6-60 Britten, "Let the florid music praise"

EXAMPLE 6-60 Continued

On rare occasions we find a melodic event that invites a final nuance even though the final harmonic change has already happened. This situation is worth noting, since special handling is required:

EXAMPLE 6-61 Beethoven, "Nimm sie hin denn diese Lieder"

The last five measures of this landmark song-cycle are over a tonic pedal point, so there is no question of harmonic interest here. The final statement of the signature tune, however, needs a significant ritard to finish things in style.

EXAMPLE 6-62 Brahms, "O kühler Wald"

An unusual orchestration for this very brief postlude features no harmonic activity, but the sol-mi-do melody in the bass needs to be enjoyed and followed with a leisurely arpeggio, which must be as warm and refreshing as the forest addressed in the song.

EXAMPLE 6-63 Mahler, "Ich bin der Welt abhanden gekommen"

Mahler is very fond of using an appoggiatura and its resolution to portray timelessness. His finale to the immense "Lied von der Erde" ends with multiple vocal statements of "ewig" ("forever") using this device. In this celebrated song from the *Rückertlieder* it is the pianist who depicts eternity. Again we have a melodic cadence which dictates our nuance, although harmonically we have already finished the experience.

Seven

The Bother of Balance

I hated writing this chapter. Some thoughts about balance between partners must be included in a book such as this, but since the performer cannot be in two places at once, helpful guidance can at best take the form of unscientific suggestions and intuitive guesswork. This text has attempted so far to be analytical and objective with its advice, but counsel about good balance can defy that goal so easily.

Most performers are intent on "trying out" the hall before a concert; I insist on this myself. But what are we really gleaning from this rehearsal or practice session? For the pianist, it is absolutely critical to learn the eccentricities of the instrument she will play in performance, for we know that no two pianos are exactly alike. For both performers, the need to discover the logistics of entering and leaving the stage can be met; lighting can be discussed, as well as various other backstage issues—water, music stands, dressing rooms . . . you name it. But the ability to gauge balance—even if it were a precise science—is an impossibility in an empty hall. Friends can be recruited to help, but this attempt too can be maddening. If the pianist brings another pianist, the singer on stage is convinced that she is being drowned and that there is a vast non-singer conspiracy against her being heard at all; similarly, a singer in the audience offering an opinion as to balance does not inspire the trust of the pianist on the stage, for it is probably a given that pianists are always too loud in the opinion of such a person. The problem of proper balance clearly remains unsolved.

For me one rule is inviolate and never to be compromised: If I cannot hear my partner, I am certainly too loud. All my concerns and techniques for achieving perfect ensemble are futile if my partner is not easily audible to me. As I stressed earlier, I must be in touch with breaths, diction issues, tempo adjustments, virtually any emergency that might arise, and all of these elements require subtle detection which bad or even imperfect balance on the stage would never allow.

At the same time that we are exercising caution not to overwhelm our partners, we must also remember that we are custodians of the composer's whole canvas, not simply an au-pair for our soloist. When balance issues arise, we cannot quickly convert the keyboard part to a soft dynamic and then consider the problem solved; something must replace the decibels we have had to reduce. Non-musical parallels can illustrate this point well: One can eat a sixteen-ounce marbled T-bone steak, or get the same protein from an eight-ounce lean filet mignon; one drop of expensive, potent perfume can easily replace two sprays of workaday cologne. With well-defined pianism, clean articulation, pedaling that maintains clarity, and voicing that highlights what is most important *within* the keyboard part, we can afford to lower the dynamic once or even twice and retain the role originally intended for the piano.

Keep Your Lid On

A word or two about the position of the lid of the piano is called for at this point. Just as the soft pedal should be used primarily for coloring rather than balance control, the question of raising the instrument's lid has little to do with volume and everything to do with clarity, color, and profile. With larger chamber works, particularly for three or more players, there is no argument: the full stick is always used. This position accomplishes two things: first, it enables the pianist to be understood through rich or dense textures, often honoring the composer's request for enormous amounts of sound; second, it visually influences the mindset of both pianist and audience. The piano's role in these quasi-symphonic chamber works is sometimes that of the hero against the odds, similar to the relationship between soloist and orchestra in the concerto literature. The fully raised lid of the instrument displays ego and a protagonist's mentality, both just as important in collaboration—*when it is appropriate*—as is modest, self-effacing playing in other circumstances.

At the other end of the spectrum, I believe the lid of the piano should *never* be closed completely. Performing with a closed lid would be tantamount to gagging a public speaker. Soloists (and teachers!) who are obsessed with balance may believe this solves the problem, but all it accomplishes is muddying and confusing the pianism, actually making many a pianist play louder as she strives for clarity and focused tone. Even an opening of four or six inches will allow vastly improved projection of the piano's tone. Knowing I might need this minimal lift, I have often traveled with a small block of wood, since most American instruments are equipped with only full- and medium-length sticks.

Another aspect of this piano lid discussion comes into play with vocal music because singers, unlike their instrumental cousins, are free to employ more physicality while performing. They may elect to use the horizontal surface of the lid with their hands or arms, perhaps to relax, perhaps for stability, or simply to create different physical attitudes during a recital. In addition to all our acoustic concerns when discussing balance and the role of the lid of the piano, with singers care must be taken that the height of the lid does not inadvertently create awkward poses, asymmetrically raised shoulders, or anything visual that would distract from the music-making itself. Fashions change continually, and as I write these lines, it has become more common, even fashionable to raise the lid completely, regardless of the collaborating instrument's projection, physical stature, or the nature of the composition itself. For some, the feelings are very intense on this subject, far more passionate than simple conviction. For me, as long as the lid of the instrument is not entirely closed, I can manage. I have many non-negotiable beliefs, things I would go to the wall to defend, but the lid of my instrument is not one of them.

Special Problems

Certain conditions may exist which should automatically alert the concerned collaborator to special balance problems.

Register

Most instruments we might partner have one area that is weaker than another. Whether it be a protracted event in this register, or a quick visit, the pianist must be careful to allow for a significant change in her partner's ability to project in this part of the range. For voice, one might think it would be the singer's lowest notes, but I have found that the middle range is more frequently the problem; it is too high for healthy, acceptable chest voice singing and too low for the natural increased projection of higher notes to "kick in." For string instruments, it is inevitably the two middle strings of their four. With flute, it is the lowest fifth of the range, and conversely with bassoon, the highest fifth. If oboe, clarinet, and all the brass instruments have weak areas in their ranges, I have yet to find them! These lucky partnerships are easier than all the others when it comes to balance; not only is their projection consistent throughout their ranges, but the difference in their timbre from the piano's is so extreme that we need not worry in most cases.

EXAMPLE 7-1 Schumann, "Frühlingsnacht"

A particularly frustrating challenge to good balance arises when both instruments are in the same octave at the same dynamic. The probability of overwhelming the soloist is at its greatest in this instance. When this song is sung by a man, the octave displacement between the voice and the pianist's repeated chords makes balancing the two far easier; with a woman's voice, particular care must be taken to prune the density of these chords or the audience will hear a piano concerto with incidental and occasional singing.

If the pianist is careful enough to begin each measure's series of repeated chords softly, there is room to observe Schumann's crescendo and still not overwhelm the voice. This crescendo is the point, after all, not some absolute dynamic. In addition, use extremely bright voicing, favoring the top of the right hand and never allowing other chord tones to become thick or emphasized.

EXAMPLE 7-2 Schubert, "Fischerweise"

Here is another, very similar example. Again, much depends on the gender of the singer. With a female, all of the music in the right hand must be played at a discreet volume; the voice is singing lower pitches than the piano and only a third away. Of course when the singer is momentarily absent, the right hand can come quickly and briefly to the fore, but otherwise we must use left-hand material to entertain and tell the story. With a male voice, everything is reversed: the bass must remain leggiero, while the right hand can enjoy its juicy thirds and the lifestyle praised in the poem.

Speed and Words

It stands to reason that with extremely rapid passagework in the soloist's part, the volume produced will be less—at all dynamics—than the score might suggest. Agility requires less cholesterol in the sound, less baggage on the athlete's back, and the pianist must allow for this. With vocal music, patter songs in any language will always limit the singer's volume; with so much text to negotiate, the singer's mouth will obviously never be open for very long.

EXAMPLE 7-3 Brahms, "Röslein dreie in der Reihe"

Only a dozen of the singer's notes are long enough to allow for serious sound production, and the bulk of this giddy song is the speed of speech, if not faster. Add to that an accompaniment that has an impulse with every syllable and the German language's consonant predominance, and you have a balance problem ready to happen. Extremely delicate, lean playing is required, with the subtlest pedaling imaginable.

EXAMPLE 7-4 Wolf, "Waldmädchen"

EXAMPLE 7-4 Continued

for - dert mich zum lust' - gen Wir - bel - tanz,

This hyperactive sprite speaks faster than she flies, and certainly faster than she thinks! True, she has a very high fairy voice, but her keyboard partner has both hands in the treble clef and has many more notes to play than she. The song's total dynamic scheme is immense, to suggest the territory she covers in her flight as well as her enormous ego; this large scope must be preserved. The loud keyboard outbursts, however, must be reserved for the piano solos—and there are many—whereas during the singing extreme care must be paid to balance. The soprano's mouth is open only for microseconds at a time.

EXAMPLE 7-5 Francoeur, Cello sonata in E, ii

EXAMPLE 7-5 Continued

Here is the instrumental version of the same problem. The cellist will doubtless use a feather-light spiccato for this very brilliant movement and astonish us with his virtuosity. Played on a modern piano, the continuo part could present an obstacle to this. The pianist must have the delicate, dryer sounds of a harpsichord in mind throughout this movement, particularly in the right hand. I want my cellist partner to be completely unaware of me as we perform this.

String Specifics

Of course, even a novice would know that pizzicato needs careful attention for good balance with the piano. Try the second vivace in the second movement of Brahms's second violin sonata —what a lot of twos!—and try to keep the amount of sound *under* what the fiddle is producing. This is no easy matter, as Brahms's piano writing is never thin.

Less obvious is the fact that double-stops (octaves included) can produce slightly *less* sound than single notes on all string instruments; this effect is counterintuitive for a pianist, since it is the opposite for our instrument. This surprising fact remains true regardless of register or dynamic. Of course, sometimes the double-stop writing is uncomfortable or awkward enough that string players appreciate a bit of bad balance (i.e., the piano a bit on the loud side) to give them some camouflage as they negotiate an unidiomatic passage. In the same Brahms movement, just before the final vivace, there are two double-stops which most violinists wish were briefer in duration. We can help at the piano by creating the warmest possible envelope in which to play these.

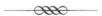

EXAMPLE 7-6 Brahms, Violin sonata in G, op.78, ii

Visit these measures of double-stops for the fiddle in its middle range in this movement. Raise the violin part an octave or remove the double-stop and the problem disappears. As Brahms has scored it, however, the pianist must take care not to allow the sumptuousness of the idiom and the key to produce too generous a dynamic scheme; the violin has the principal thematic material after all.

EXAMPLE 7-7 Bartok, Romanian Dance #5

Another balance issue for this family of instruments is harmonics. No intelligent composer would expect sonorous piano playing during these special string sounds. Whatever the dynamic specified for the pianist, they must be read through special, prudent lenses; the string player cannot force or drive a harmonic passage. The glassy resonance that harmonics create cannot compete with rich pianism.

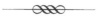

EXAMPLE 7-8 Strauss, Violin sonata, ii

The last specific string balance issue is, of course, *con sordina*, the use of the mute. It is self-evident that care must be taken when you are accompanying this altered string color. However, bear in mind that even with the mute, a significant range of dynamics is still available to the player, just as with *una corda* passages on the piano. Rather than thinking only softly or carefully, I would suggest thinking sweetly and purely. Most composers employ this color for heavenly, ethereal moments, not necessarily the softest ones.

Voice Specifics

Some vowels inherently project more easily than others. Very closed versions of [e] (sehr, été, venti), [i] (sieh, fils, Mimi), [y] (müde, du in french), and [o] (Moos, eau, Roma) have so much focus when pronounced purely and correctly that even when other problematic conditions exist, good balance is not terribly difficult to achieve. If all else remains the same and the vowels are opened to [a], [ɛ], [I], or [ɔ], balance becomes an issue as focus declines. Finally, I have found the vowel [u] (Ruh, vous, fu in Italian, and too in English) to be the least projecting of all, and I am automatically extremely careful of balance when accompanying this sound. A particularity of French is, of course, the four nasal vowels; exaggerating their nasality can aid enormously in creating good balance, for the focus then approximates the very closed sounds mentioned earlier. Before giving up sonority, pianists should suggest this option to their vocal partners.

EXAMPLE 7-9 Debussy, "La chevelure"

The climax of this very sensuous song is absurdly idealistic——not only in what it is describing, but when it comes to dynamics and balance. The mezzo-soprano is only in her middle range, and yet the composer asks for fortissimo from the pianist. Luckily, the word "songe" can be slightly over-nasalized, alleviating the problem somewhat. Pianists can also help by reducing their dynamic immediately after the downbeat, playing the harmonic reiterations "inside" the initial chord.

EXAMPLE 7-10 Canteloube, "Brezairola"

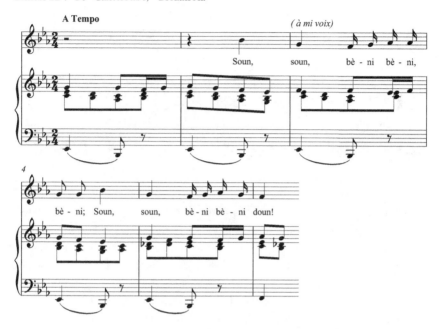

This enchanting lullaby from Canteloube's huge collection of Auvergne folksong arrangements is performed with piano almost as often as with orchestra. There is a predominance here of words with [u] sounds, creating assonance and internal rhymes which would put any child to sleep. "Soun" and "doun" can produce only so much sound before they lose their purity and individual color. The accompaniments throughout this collection are luxurious, colorful, and generously chromatic, but in this case the pianist must take great care to allow tenderness and transparency at all times.

EXAMPLE 7-11 Ginastera, "Arrorró"

This folk-lullaby is in an ABA form, and the repeated a section is begun with the singer humming wordlessly. I don't know how phoneticians classify the sound of humming, but I am certain it requires the utmost delicacy from the pianist. Humming always has very limited possibilities for volume, and it is never used in aggressive or powerful moments; the pianist must obviously follow suit. Other instances of a hummed voice part are found in Ives's "Memories A & B," the first movement of Villa-Lobos's *Bachianas Brasilieras #5,* and Bernstein's "Nachspiel." To remind the reader: if you can't hear your partner easily, something needs to be adjusted.

In conclusion, I would emphasize again that balance is an imprecise science. There are too many variables for advice to be universal or consistent. No two artists are looking for the same internal balance with their partnership, and furthermore, empty concert halls and dead recording or rehearsal studios are not laboratories to be trusted. I suppose a top-quality recording device could be placed in the middle of the concert hall and then analyzed by both performers after a significant amount of music has been captured. Be sure to include soft and loud passages, fast and slow, different parts of the range, and piano parts that are both competitive and modest. Doing this would provide honest documentation (albeit in an empty space) of what was happening, although it would not necessarily guarantee agreement by the performers.

When ideal balance has been discovered—if there is any such thing—a pianist should immediately seek to memorize the composite sound of the volumes of this particular soloist and herself—*as it sounds when she is sitting at the piano.* The memory of the sound of this ratio is all we can really count on. This is very like practicing piano on a silent keyboard, or a singer recording with earphones on. It is the re-membered sensation that tells us we are doing things correctly. With balance, when that approved ratio is heard, we can assume things are on track.

Remember too that the piano can easily outdo any of its partners, except per-haps members of the brass family or the piccolo. Even if the pianist is certain the balance is good but hears her partner forcing to add sound, not behaving as planned by the two of you—perhaps choking to reduce the volume, or otherwise suffering and distorting what could be a marvelous performance—the balance must be reinvestigated and probably recalculated immediately. So many solutions exist without reducing the accompaniment to lackey status. Revisit my earlier remarks about substituting other qualities for volume; remember too that songs can be transposed and more appropriate repertoire can be diplomatically sug-gested, should all else fail. The bottom line? Collaboration cannot exist without flexibility; this is as important in dealing with balance as in any other aspect of performance.

EIGHT

The Steinway Philharmonic*

Introduction

As I write these lines, I am very aware of how the life of a professional collaborative pianist has changed, particularly for those who work primarily with singers. The first famous accompanist of whom I was aware was Gerald Moore. I knew of him through his witty lectures, his books, and his consistently superb recordings. I am confident that Sir Gerald could play arias as well as anyone, but the fact is that his performing career did not often require him to do so. He accompanied countless artists who sang opera, but never on recital programs. I don't know if Moore worked much with opera, but it is certainly not what comes to mind at the mention of his illustrious name. The Canadian pianist John Newmark excelled at lieder and mélodie but pretty much eschewed anything for orchestra, as did his very in-demand Viennese colleague Erik Werba. I vividly recall one of my favorite partners, soprano Judith Blegen, telling me that a certain ex-patriot American based in Switzerland, much recorded and renowned for superb collaborative work, patently refused to accompany her in an operatic encore at a European recital. (I told her she should have taken me along instead!)

That is all in the past; today everything has changed. Playing opera both in performance and in a coaching capacity has become a huge part of any collaborator's life, should he want to eat regularly and enjoy a roof over his head. There may be a handful of pianists who manage to restrict their repertoire to songs, but they would work mainly in Europe and the UK, and I suspect that even there it is becoming increasingly difficult to maintain this elite position these days. As I have said so often in these pages, the collaborator is nothing if not flexible; if the times demand orchestral playing, we will provide it, and enthusiastically so!

*Let me give full credit to my former student and now esteemed colleague Dr. Russell Miller, who coined the amusing and very appropriate title of this chapter during his doctoral studies. He has been kind enough to permit me to borrow it.

In other texts about accompanying, there is inevitably a chapter such as this, dealing with orchestral repertoire. The consistent emphasis seems to be on the pianist's *simplifying* everything, *removing any extraneous material* and concentrating on *surviving an onslaught* of unplayable arias and concerti. The italics are my own, but these are direct quotes from texts by various colleagues of previous generations. For myself, I prefer to put only the most positive of spins on this subject. These orchestral reductions are fascinating problems in what to play and how to play it. Every piece we prepare is a unique, individual creation, and no two pianists will play an aria identically. Yes, to be sure, survival is inherent in doing this well, but it should not be our primary mindset.

Professional and financial considerations aside, and joking too, playing music for orchestra is of enormous benefit to the pianist. First, since we cannot duplicate *exactly* what the orchestra plays, we are compelled to be inventive and highly creative in selecting what and how to play. Unlike a Schubert song where every note must be executed, comfortably or not, with orchestral transcriptions all is permitted and nothing is the "real thing." What a pianist chooses to play—the very notes themselves—will say more about his personal priorities than six dozen songs written originally for keyboard accompaniment.

Second, nothing can plunge a pianist into the world of colors faster than imitating an orchestra. With live performances all around him and an inexhaustible supply of recorded music today, the orchestral model is there for the listening and imitating. In this repertoire, pianists resemble organists in a way, playing instruments with multiple rows of stops. Organists have mechanical assistance and call it registration; we experiment until we have created our own "stops" and we call it orchestration. Thus we can triumph over the all-purpose, generic nature of the piano, and nothing will accelerate this process faster than playing music for orchestra. Then on another occasion, returning to accompaniments for piano, we will, it is hoped, have developed a significantly increased appetite for timbres and colors, and we may find ourselves unconsciously imagining orchestration in everything we play. What could be better?

Last—and this becomes a trifle metaphysical perhaps—the pianist playing orchestral material learns quite quickly that the symbols in front of him are just that: symbols, and not the Music itself. If there are different editions available, he can see differing ideas of how to reduce the orchestral music for only two hands. Thus the printed page, the thing we are taught to respect and revere from our earliest piano lessons, loses its status as the Document and assumes the humble role of only *one* person's *opinion* of how said Document could be represented. This is an enormous and critical change of mindset, and for many it seems much harder to achieve with music that was originally written for the piano. Nevertheless, whether we confine ourselves to the printed page or create our own transcriptions, we realize sooner or later that all the myriad instructions we strive so valiantly to obey are but symbols to guide us to the *real* music. I believe orchestral playing can hasten this realization.

In this chapter, the truth or the Document I have referred to above is the actual playing of a real orchestra. It is crucial for a pianist to acknowledge to himself that there is simply no way to perform that truth. We cannot copy the letter of the law, but we can certainly pursue its spirit. Bear in mind, however, that what one person believes that spirit to be may differ considerably from another's opinion. Both are passionate. Both are right, and both are wrong. Everything is a lie. Until a pianist embraces compromise, there can be no success in playing orchestral music. Literal, rigid perfectionists cannot exist in this world of orchestral reduction. Only when someone can say the following, unapologetically, has the path to enjoying success in this repertoire been found:

> This is the very best compromise, the best lie I could devise. I have heard the original. I have experimented sufficiently, and I feel that my version respects and preserves the salient and essential features of this music, as I hear and understand them. I deliver my version to my partner and my audience with the confidence that only pianistic comfort and guaranteed practicality can bring.

Note particularly the end of this little oath. Comfort and practicality must be part of all our decisions here. These are not always available when we practice "Erlkönig" or "Cäcilie," for we are slaves to the composer's daunting notes written originally for our instrument. To introduce labor or uncertainty into playing orchestra music when unlimited alternate choices are acceptable would be misguided or, to be blunt, stupid. I have found that the most uncanny paradox exists: when we make ourselves pianistically comfortable playing reductions, we acquire the means to sound orchestral. As the spy in *Andrea Chénier* says: *incredibile, ma vero*— unbelievable, but true!

Being Ourselves

Before proceeding in this discussion of orchestral sounds, we must make sure we never sound like a pianist. The only instrument we might imitate that sounds like a piano is . . . a piano. Without too much thought, three examples using piano in the standard aria literature occur to me:

 EXAMPLE 8-I Puccini, La canzone di Doretta, *La Rondine*

This aria's introduction is for piano solo exclusively until its last bar.

 EXAMPLE 8-2 Moore, Willow song, *The Ballad of Baby Doe*

Our heroine sits at a piano on stage and accompanies herself. This introduction too is scored for piano alone.

EXAMPLE 8-3 Strauss, Grossmächtige Prinzessin, *Ariadne auf Naxos*

The piano is very active in the chamber orchestra for which this opera is scored. In this aria, it alone accompanies the singer for the first dozen measures.

In the above examples, and anything else scored for piano, we can relax and simply be ourselves. In any other orchestration, however, anything that remotely resembles piano playing must be avoided. The geography of the keyboard—it is four feet wide after all—is a significant factor in playing the piano, but this must not play any role in performing orchestral music. Pianists plan tempi and rubato, sometimes unconsciously, based on the layout of the keyboard. Jumps are physically and psychologically expensive for a keyboard player, but not necessarily so for an orchestral instrument. Tempi or rhythmic liberties predicated on these jumps will instantly ruin any orchestral disguise. The Moore example above has a left-hand part that is ever so slightly wider in span than is comfortable; a little rhythmic elasticity solves the problem. With the Puccini introduction we encounter a brief virtuoso event which requires juicily arpeggiated chords plus a generous dynamic, and covers almost the entire keyboard. Rubato here is necessary both technically and stylistically. In other words, the expression for both of these excerpts is affected entirely by the keyboard itself, coupled with the fact that only one player is executing them in the original. A single brain can risk and enjoy taking rhythmic liberties, whereas with an orchestra the group mentality must rule. We could guess the scoring for these examples when we hear them well performed on the piano, simply because they are delivered with rhythmic freedom and individual flair, both of which would be foreign to orchestral playing.

EXAMPLE 8-4 Mozart, Chi'io mi scordi di te, concert aria, K.505

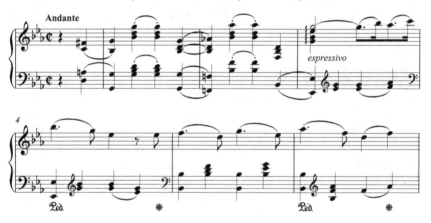

This beautiful concert aria provides a wonderful testing ground for a pianist sounding alternately like an orchestra and like himself, for it is scored for mezzo-soprano, piano solo, and orchestra. It is no easy feat to suggest the difference in timbres here. Extra projection for the piano solo and much less incisive playing for the orchestra is a good start. A bit of tasteful rubato juxtaposed with no liberty whatsoever strengthens the illusion of piano versus orchestra. Notes that stubbornly refuse to revert to the orchestral background color might be omitted or moved an octave away.

On Your Mark. . . .

Leaving behind us the comfort zone of sounding like a piano, we now consider the specific sounds of various instruments. An important caveat to keep in mind is: we are not imitating what the player actually does to create these sounds; we are imitating the end result of his actions; the actual sounds, as we perceive them, are our goal. Imagine tasting something, loving it, having no recipe, and experimenting in the kitchen until that taste is duplicated. This is our task. Do not be tricked into thinking you can experience lips on a mouthpiece or fingertips on a string. We are pianists imitating only the results of these actions.

Whenever a new piece for orchestra is to be learned, be it an aria, a concerto, or even a whole opera or oratorio, it is imperative to know the orchestration *before* beginning to practice the piece. If time permits, studying the full score and listening to recordings are clearly one's primary aids to this end. Of these two, I believe the latter is much more helpful, especially for pianists who are less experienced with orchestral reductions. A simple orchestration by Handel, Mozart, or Rossini is not difficult to "hear" as one reads the conductor's score, but looking at more complex scores by Verdi, Puccini, and particularly those of Wagner, Mahler, and Strauss, can stymie all but experienced conductors. Listening tells us more of what we need to know. If a middle-voice string figure is for cello and the listener has guessed viola, that will not affect how he deals with it at the piano. Similarly guessing oboe instead of English horn is no tragedy for the pianist-imitator. Do remember, however: we are listening to a recorded version to learn the orchestration, *not* the tempo nor the expression. We are not copying the music-making, only assembling the materials.

As one listens, the piano score is open and ready to be marked within an inch of its life. Each pianist needs to devise his own shorthand which will instantly tell him all he needs to know. Here is what I use:

Stgs	strings
WW	winds
BR	brass
Perc	percussion
PZ	pizzicato
Arc	arco

When solo instruments are heard, I use Fl, Ob, Cl, Fg, Tpt, Trb, Hn, Vln, Vla, VC, CB, Hp, Timp, and Pf (i.e., the piano).

Do not be proud; don't rely on your memory—mark everything on the music. As a collaborator, you will learn more and more repertoire all the time, and it might be years before you encounter this piece again. Since the orchestration will never change, why do this very time-consuming homework a second time?

Sustaining the Sound

One very fundamental difference between what we are playing and what we are imitating is the involuntary decay inherent in the mechanics of the piano.

EXAMPLE 8-5 Mozart, "Dalla sua pace," *Don Giovanni*

EXAMPLE 8-5 Continued

EXAMPLE 8-6 Puccini, "Signore, ascolta," *Turandot*

It often is necessary to re-strike a note or even an entire chord in order to maintain the sustaining quality of the orchestra, regardless of the orchestration. Doing so will of course introduce a rhythmic impulse which is not in the orchestra, but a chord that is no longer audible or capable of support is not the composer's intention either. If you feel the sustained quality is of paramount importance, then re-striking is a must, but when and how you do so will make all the difference. Sometimes simply re-striking the bass note can do the job; other times the whole chord is required. Tempo is a big factor here, for the slower the music, the more the decay of the piano will ruin things. In a passage with moving harmonies in the upper voices but only a single long bass note, the ear must continually monitor whether enough of the root is still sounding to render the various chords above it complete and well-balanced. Repeating the bass once or even twice might be necessary, lest its absence render the harmonies unstable or unsupported.

Strings

We need our warmest, least percussive sound for strings. Flat, fleshy fingers and minimum articulation are the best choice; any sound of hammers or keys would be foreign. This is probably the sumptuous playing you would use for keyboard music by Brahms (minus the rubato, of course!). In his second sonata for clarinet and piano, the trio section of the second movement seems a fine role model for how to suggest strings at the piano. A similar example is the slow movement of the same composer's third violin sonata. Indeed, strings are what I imagine when I play these classic chamber music moments.

EXAMPLE 8-7 Mozart, "Un aura amorosa," *Così fan tutte*

EXAMPLE 8-8 Weber, "Leise, leise," *Der Freischutz*

EXAMPLE 8-9 Massenet, "Il est doux, il est bon," *Hérodiade*

All these examples are scored for strings. With all orchestral playing, but particularly with string passages, additional richness is easily obtained with adding a lower octave to the bass line. Not only is this probably the truth—remember that the double bass sounds an octave lower than written—but one's playing acquires added cholesterol when one moves lower on the keyboard, always an asset for rich string imitations.

It will probably follow that by adding lower octaves in the left hand, some voices will need to be transferred to the right hand. Here is where personal priorities begin to come into play. One pianist may feel that the added depth is worth the loss of the tenor voice where it really sounds, or worth the extra work for the right hand as it takes on an additional voice; another pianist may be quite adamant about the viola part remaining where it is, and for him, adding octaves is not worth the loss of this original register. A pianist must feel passionate about his decisions, mindful that others will have different priorities but convinced of his choices nonetheless.

If octaves are added, be careful that they begin and end in reasonable places, places the composer could have chosen. The voice-leading you invent must make sense. As always, your ear is the ultimate test when you add these octaves. Adding them too low on the keyboard can introduce density and darkness reminiscent of Russian male chorus repertoire, thus destroying a credible imitation of strings. Playing Handel's "Ombra mai fu" from *Serse* in its original key of F begs for added octaves in the left hand to sound orchestral and to avoid resembling keyboard music of this period. If it is transposed down to E-flat, many pianists may still find these octaves acceptable in sound, but it's becoming increasingly questionable. Transpose but one more step to D-flat, and the piano now sounds like a newly discovered transcription by Rachmaninoff, and Handel has completely disappeared.

Tremolo

String tremolo is encountered constantly when we play orchestral music. On the piano, repeating a note is not at all the most comfortable motion we make, whereas rotating the wrist can be done endlessly. Thus a chord alternating upper and lower notes in the hand has become a vital part of any pianist's physical vocabulary, and we call it *tremolo*. This alternation, which allows sonority and busyness to comfortably coexist, is very different from what strings actually do when playing their tremolos. With strings there is no alternation, only the repetition of a note or notes. At the beginning of a string tremolo, all the notes in a chord are heard simultaneously. If the alternation that pianists must use to imitate the strings' gesture is too predominant initially, we have a moment in a Beethoven piano sonata, not a Puccini aria. We must strike the complete chord and then tremolo "inside" that initial impact. If the whole chord is unreachable, strike the highest and lowest poles and then add the remaining notes inside what you have done. It's a bit akin to striking the initial chord outside imaginary parentheses and then "tremolo-ing" inside them for as long as necessary. Sometimes the upper or lower voices of a tremolo transcribed for piano may be visually far to the right, because of accidentals or perhaps because the soloist's line requires more horizontal space.

Be careful to mark the score so as to provide the complete chord for your eye at the very beginning of the tremolo.

EXAMPLE 8-10 Massenet, "Adieu, notre petite table," *Manon*

EXAMPLE 8-11 Giordano, "Nemico della patria," *Andrea Chénier*

EXAMPLE 8-12 Wagner, "O du, mein holder Abendstern," *Tannhaüser*

EXAMPLE 8-13 Rossini, "Una voce poco fa," *Il Barbiere di Siviglia*

EXAMPLE 8-14 Mozart, "Hai già vinta la causa," *Le Nozze di Figaro*

 EXAMPLE 8-14 Continued

Be particularly careful of tremolos that are very high on the piano. Even in the best of hands these can take on a honky-tonk sound that no string section could ever imagine. Using only the inside notes of such a chord for the tremolo can often improve the imitation immensely.

 EXAMPLE 8-15 Puccini, "Donde lieta uscì," *La Boheme*

Remember that a tremolo's function is to provide excitement *inside* the material; it is never important on its own. In achieving this "inside" sound, the middle of the keyboard can be our best friend. The octaves immediately above and below middle C have the least danger of escaping outside of the parentheses I am suggesting. The sound in these octaves is inherently more generic, less brilliant. Here is an alternative solution for this same moment in Mimi's aria.

EXAMPLE 8-16 Puccini, "Donde lieta uscì," *La Bohème*

The slow tempo allows this option and maintains practicality despite the jumps. There is no danger of a strident sound in the right hand as it tremolos, and the parentheses are created automatically because of the register changes. Using this method requires us to "sneak" the tremolo in—the audience must think it was there from the initial impact of the chord. This is truly smoke and mirrors in their best sense.

There may be occasions when the harmonic rhythm and the tempo of the piece combine to make tremolos awkward and impractical. Worse, to do them as transcribed would violate the principle of excitement *within* the music. We need the excitement, but it can be restricted or transferred to the more stable hand, allowing the busier hand to play the larger shape of the music rather than sound like a nightmare of a tremolo etude. Tremolo is not difficult for the strings, so we must take great care to prevent the foreign element of labor to contaminate the sound of string tremolo when it is executed on the piano.

EXAMPLE 8-17 Mozart, "Misero! O sogno o son desto?" concert aria, K.431

Pizzicato

Pizzicato is also a big part of string imitation. Take care that all plucked impulses are the same length, regardless of the printed rhythmic value assigned by the composer. My own pizzicato imitation consists of no voicing whatsoever and not much focus in the tone. I achieve this (when I do) with a fairly flabby hand and minimal concentration in my fingertips. I have no idea how a string player's fingers feel when he is playing pizzicato—nor is that my concern; I am imitating only the resulting sound as I hear it filtered through the piano. The pedal is absolutely taboo, and thus the uniform length of the notes is controlled exclusively by the fingers. To reiterate about marking the score: every chord that might make me ask myself, "Is this pizzicato or arco?" is marked accordingly in my music *before* I set about learning the piece. Obviously this orchestration will never change, so this an excellent investment of a pianist's time.

🔊 EXAMPLE 8-18 Mozart, "Voi che sapete," *Le Nozze di Figaro*

EXAMPLE 8-19 Rossini, "Cruda sorte," *L'Italiana in Algeri*

EXAMPLE 8-19 Continued

Here are two excellent examples of music employing a significant amount of pizzicato. In the Mozart, the strings pluck for the entire piece; their bows are in their laps. Remember not to favor the top of these chords when voicing them. With Isabella's hilarious cabaletta the first eight measures are very fast pizzicato only. Note that the quarter-note downbeat of the fifth bar is no longer than all the eighth notes preceding it. The player cannot control the length of a plucked note, so neither should the pianist.

Occasionally we must execute sustained playing simultaneously with pizzicato, and this task can be particularly daunting when only one hand must deal with both articulations. Here I would choose the shortest length possible for the pizzicato voices. A tiny window of opportunity is thereby created for the pedal to be brought into play, but only *after* the plucked impulse is gone. This maneuver is as challenging a task for the right foot as it is for the hands, but the impression it creates can be stunning and is well worth the trouble when one is eager to create the best imitation possible.

EXAMPLE 8-20 Mozart, "Ruhe sanft, mein holdes Leben," *Zaïde*

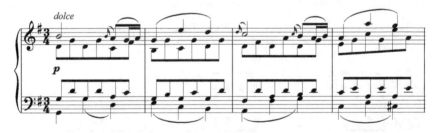

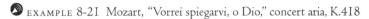 EXAMPLE 8-21 Mozart, "Vorrei spiegarvi, o Dio," concert aria, K.418

Warning! In far too many piano/vocal scores, anything pizzicato is printed with a wavy line in front of it, indicating arpeggiation. I have no idea when or how this notational tradition began, but it is to be avoided like the plague. Strike these notes together; we are always imitating a world-class orchestra's string section, one which watches the maestro intently, always playing perfectly together.

Woodwinds

Rather than the plump, warm tone used for the strings, a very focused and quick finger attack is an excellent way to imitate this section of the orchestra. I hope my woodwind colleagues and friends will not be offended; remember, we are seeking only how the piano can represent the result of their actions. Yes, the winds are playing with warmth, but in order to capture their timbres and differentiate them from other instruments, I feel a steely, cool, and very articulate finger technique works best on the piano.

I have never found a way to be specific about the sound of a particular woodwind on the piano. Flute is light and bright, clarinet and bassoon have wonderful low notes, and oboe probably projects a bit more than its cousins, but in general the register in which we are playing will suggest the specific instrument to the audience. Be content to sound like a woodwind; which wind in particular is not important for the pianist-imitator.

Playing very cleanly, but not without pedal, is also an important feature of woodwind imitation. No instrument in this family plays more than one note at a time, and the mechanics of these instruments—the keys, the holes, things not found with string instruments—ask for a cleaner, leaner articulation. Be careful to lift the finger precisely as the next finger is depressed. You might want to play the same passage as if it were orchestrated for strings for the sake of comparison and to decide if your articulation is sufficient to imply a woodwind sound.

Beyond copying the sound of this instrumental family, there is a significant difference between the mindset of the wind player and that of his string colleague. This too affects how the pianist proceeds. Each player in a wind section is really a soloist; there are not a dozen others playing the same notes with him as would be the case with strings. This difference is crucial, because it introduces an individual ego as well as psychological pressure to everything winds do. For the imitator at the piano, when this solo mentality is combined with the penetrating finger technique described earlier, everything for winds will feel less generic, less homogenized in the hand than any passage for strings. One would naturally assume this attitude for woodwind solos, but it applies to homophonic group wind passages as well. If eight or ten fingers are involved, each one feels a soloist's mentality; each one is aware of its own linear adventure, and the result is unique, quite unlike most piano music.

EXAMPLE 8-22 Mozart, "Secondate, aurette amiche," *Così fan tutte*

A pianist would probably need only to perform this duet in rehearsals for a complete Così, but for our purposes it provides a splendid laboratory for getting acquainted with woodwind playing. This serenade from act 2 is scored exclusively for winds. As a result, one's fingers are never quite relaxed from first note to last.

Remember that each finger is a soloist with ego, line, and contrapuntal adventure on his music stand. Familiar pianistic hand positions must not seduce us into ever feeling casual with wind playing.

EXAMPLE 8-23 Verdi, "Willow song," *Otello*

Here is another excellent exercise for the pianist in wind playing. The long introduction to Desdemona's scene is thirty measures entirely for reeds, foreshadowing the depressed, gloomy song to follow. I offer no new information for this example, just the challenge to make the listener confidently guess "winds" when asked about Verdi's orchestration.

EXAMPLE 8-24 Puccini, "In questa reggia," *Turandot*

EXAMPLE 8-24 Continued

un   gri - do di - spe - ra - to ri - so - nò

The introductory section of this monologue is scored for winds; the strings first enter only at the 4/8 tempo change many bars later. The imperious nature of this heroine and the Chinese atmosphere desired may be what inspired Puccini to use this special sound of winds for her first notes in the opera. These measures are easily played; they are child's play technically. But to create a wind sound, each finger feels only one impulse at a time in each of the several lines. When the strings enter, an entirely different pianist is heard.

EXAMPLE 8-25 Mozart, "Voi che sapete," *Le Nozze di Figaro*

We looked at this example earlier with regard to pizzicato. Now revisit this brief masterpiece and be aware that everything that is sustained—everything!—is a woodwind. The combination of flabby, unvoiced fingers for the string pizzicato and concentrated, very voiced fingers for the winds makes the orchestration here as magical as Mozart's notes themselves.

EXAMPLE 8-26 Ravel, "La flûte enchantée," *Shéhérazade*

The title says it all—a song for voice, flute, and orchestra. Here we consider the final two sections of the piece. As the tempo downshifts, the orchestra gradually evaporates until only flute and voice remain. With such a minimal texture, every detail is exposed, and the notion of a woodwind needing to breathe enters the picture. If we want to fully replicate the flute, there would be brief silences at all the breathing points. With string orchestrations or with repertoire for piano, one can phrase without introducing silence, but not so with woodwinds.

The Brass Family

Transferred to the piano, the brass instruments share the pressurized mindset of the winds in that only one player plays each line. Also similar to the winds, these instruments have mechanics—here valves and slides instead of keys and holes—and they too play only one note at a time. The clear articulation used for winds therefore holds true here as well. The brass sound, however, is obviously very different from that of the woodwinds. The golden overtones of these instruments are best captured with a flat-fingered warm tone from the pianist. I imagine a dash or tenuto on each note, particularly in melodic playing, and I allow the pedal to assist me with the sustaining of each sound. If these were winds or strings, I would be careful to use a finger legato, whereas with brass a slight non-legato, albeit with pedal, creates the sound we need. Again, dear brass colleagues, this is not how you play; it is only how we copy you at the piano.

EXAMPLE 8-27 Bizet, "Je dis que rien ne m'épouvante," *Carmen*

Try playing this two ways: First use an orthodox fingering in the right hand. The warmth of this key and this register, combined with beautiful legato, will imply a viola or cello section playing the tune. Now try using only one finger consecutively in the right hand for every note in the tune. Doing this will, of course, result in the dashes I spoke of earlier. As I have said, everything about imitating instruments is subjective and purely personal; for me, the dashes in the right hand articulation create the feeling and sound of a solo horn. Be sure to include the ego of the first horn as well as the intensity that results from this solo being fairly high in the instrument's range.

EXAMPLE 8-28 Donizetti, "Povero Ernesto!" *Don Pasquale*

A similar example, but this time we encounter a trumpet solo. It is wonderfully unusual to have a soft, lovesick cavatina introduced by an instrument that is normally associated with fanfares. Again, think one note at a time for articulation, particularly when many notes are in a single hand position. Think the mindset of a soloist in a naked and unaccustomed role. Without attention to a special articulation (dashes), this will never pass muster as a trumpet.

EXAMPLE 8-29 Mozart, "Per pietà," *Così fan tutte*

EXAMPLE 8-29 Continued

This is another horn example, a pair of horns actually, and with much faster notes. While the soprano might prefer a very fast tempo, the horns' requirements must be taken into consideration as well. Even though the pianist can easily furnish a breakneck speed, it would be dishonest to accustom the singer and the audience to a tempo the horns would not be able to provide in the original. Again, no disrespect intended, but as we imitate these horns, we must show that they are not clarinets or violas. Each note must be clearly and cleanly articulated, even in this allegro passagework; the combination of golden and fast is unusual and the tempo and articulation must exemplify this.

Harp

Rewriting music scored for harp to be played on the piano will rarely be necessary, for the two instruments are closely related, certainly more so than any other instruments in the orchestra. Remember, however, that legato is impossible here; plucking and glissando are our only choices. The pianist imitating harp should feel he is playing Scarlatti on the keyboard and Debussy with his right foot. This combination creates the specific sound required here.

A harp exclusive is its *laissez vibrer* aspect. Until a string is touched again, its sound will remain. This "afterglow" is perhaps why the impressionist composers are so partial to this instrument. It adds special resonance and a soft vagueness to all it touches. The player must consciously touch the vibrating strings to stop the sound. The composer may dictate precise cutoffs, but these specific instructions are found primarily in contemporary scores.

Here, and only here, my earlier remarks about ignoring instructions to arpeggiate can be disregarded. Harpists often roll chords and octaves, with or without instructions from the composer; it has become almost their signature attitude. So we too at the piano, once we learn that something is for harp, can treat ourselves to this same tradition. Be aware, however, that a harp is a most gentle instrument, and this added arpeggiation would be heard only if the total instrumentation were either harp solo or minimal enough that the harp could project easily above everything else.

EXAMPLE 8-30 Puccini, "Donde lieta uscì," *La Bohème*

Harp permeates this aria—Mimì's loveliness calls for it. In the final cadence, knowing that this is for harp solo, we see the score with specific eyes. The chord, if arpeggiated, would be audible to the listener, since almost nothing else is happening simultaneously. The pianist must not change the pedal for the second eighth note, since a change would necessitate the harpist's having to touch all six notes rather quickly to stop the sound, and this action is far too fussy. True, the sound is not clean, but perhaps that is precisely why Puccini has chosen the harp. The low dynamic permits this intermingling of these harmonies without creating mud.

EXAMPLE 8-31 Bellini, "O quante volte," *I Capuleti ed i Montecchi*

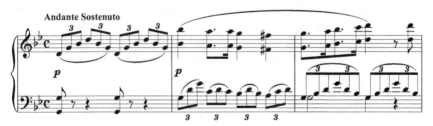

EXAMPLE 8-31 Continued

EXAMPLE 8-32 Rossini, "Willow song," *Otello*

A quick look at either of these bel canto arias, and we might guess they are for piano accompaniment. In both cases the left hand's pattern is stereotypically pianistic. The scalar passages in the Rossini are totally keyboard-esque, as are the octaves in the melody of the Bellini. These are pianist-composers scoring for harp solo, using materials they know well. If these actually were for piano, the player would be careful to change the pedal whenever the harmonies change. This is normal performance practice and offers a romantic but clean and clear texture, rather like a nocturne by Field or Chopin. But these are not for piano! There is no possibility of the harpist's dampening the already played notes fast enough to be clean, given the tempi required here. At the piano we must make sure our audience knows which instrument is really playing. The materials are so pianistic that only wet pedaling can imply the harp as the featured soloist.

EXAMPLE 8-33 Puccini, "O mio babbino caro," *Gianni Schicchi*

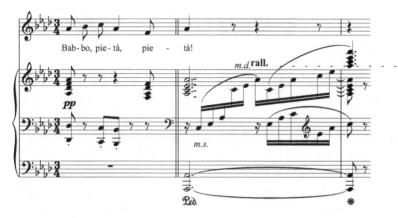

This well-known aria also seems tailor-made for the piano. Everything feels familiar, idiomatic. We can pedal generously, liberally. Don't we wish every aria were so comfortable? At the final cadence, there is time for the harpist to touch the strings and make silence after the first "Babbo, pietà, pietà"; at the piano we follow suit. The final phrase is harp solo, so we treat this just as we did the Boheme aria above.

Remember that the harp is a soloist within the orchestra. If the sixteenth notes of this aria were for the cello section (compare this with the left hand in Micaela's aria from *Carmen*), rubato would be impossible, lest all the cellos not agree. Here in the realm of the soloist, the harpist can make subtle rubati, be they for technical or expressive reasons, while staying comfortably with the conductor and the rest of the orchestra at all times.

Percussion

Pianists need not be concerned with this large family of instruments too often. Even so, if an effect is deemed important, no less attention should be paid to these more unusual colors and effects than to any other. Their use is inherently theatrical, and finding ways to imitate them can be an amusing and adventurous process. A particularly important reminder here: we are imitating the effect that an instrument makes, not what is actually being played.

Timpani

As we know, timpani are instruments with pitch, and it is always astounding to watch timpanists tune while other music is being played in the orchestra. Nevertheless, if we imitate timpani on the piano using too defined a pitch, the effect and atmosphere of these drums are lost. Normally timpani is transcribed for the second octave below middle C on the piano, but I have often found that register to be too pitch-specific for a convincing imitation. The lower we go on the piano, the less distinct the pitch, and in this case I would consider that descent desirable.

It is important to remember too that the fast repetition of a single pitch which can be achieved with alternating sticks is most easily executed on the piano with alternating pitches, normally an octave apart. But the pianist's alternation must never become audible or the point of the gesture. Strike the opening timpani note and add the alternation in a minimally articulated, parenthetical way, as was suggested for string tremolo. Or choose to strike both the low and high notes simultaneously and sneak the alternation in afterward. A generous use of pedal is also essential to create the desired impression.

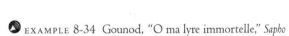

EXAMPLE 8-34 Gounod, "O ma lyre immortelle," *Sapho*

EXAMPLE 8-35 Verdi, "E sogno o realtà?" *Falstaff*

Here are two timpani solos from the standard operatic repertoire. Note that both sound more timpani-like if dropped an octave from what the piano reductions suggest. Try these in the register as printed and you will immediately hear how they resemble a piano sonata by Liszt or Weber. With the Verdi, we have the clear advantage of beginning the timpani's B-flat loudly, so that folding in the octave alternation is an easy matter. With the Gounod the rumble of thunder must begin softly enough to seem distant, but the initial impulse must be struck loudly enough to permit camouflaging the alternation that follows.

EXAMPLE 8-36 Verdi, "Re dell'abisso, affrettati!" *Un ballo in maschera*

Occasionally a timpani solo will be transcribed exactly as played, as in this example. Again, moving things an octave down creates the "right" sound. Depending on the tempo, these two flourishes of four G's could be played without alternation (and a dependable fingering!), or the pianist might choose to substitute alternation in order to guarantee all four impulses' being heard. The extremely low dynamic and nakedness of the timpani's solos here make this risky without the alternation. (Compare our freedom to play whatever we'd like here to the scary introduction to Wolf's Italian song "Ihr jungen Leute," where we can change nothing and yet must achieve a similar timpani effect. Personally, I'd rather do the opera excerpt!)

Gong, Cymbal, Bass Drum, Snare Drum

With these instruments we need to use the absolute lowest register of the piano to avoid any semblance of pitch. Apart from this counsel, it is difficult to offer generic advice, since each instance will be unique. Maximum imagination and creativity is required here.

EXAMPLE 8-37 Mahler, "Das irdische Leben," *Des Knaben Wunderhorn*

In the orchestrated version of this *Knaben Wunderhorn* song, the last note is a gong solo. Mahler saw this is as a chilling way to paint the horror of a child's starving to death. In addition to being pitchless, the gong can resonate forever with metallic overtones while we contemplate the tragedy. In the original piano version of this song, with a single B-flat scarcely more than two octaves below middle C, none of this feeling is evoked; it is far, far too mainstream a sound. Playing the lowest possible cluster of half-tones may not be the literal truth, but it has never failed to send chills up and down my spine. It further obscures the pitch, and best of all, piano music of this period never sounds like this.

Continuo

I consider this combination of two or three instruments as a single instrument to be imitated. Achieving a believable imitation of continuo is as important for playing baroque arias and sonatas as replicating the cymbal is for evoking a marching band. Given the fact that in this period a composer's options for orchestration were very limited, to neglect this sound would be to remove an important and necessary color, thereby reducing the contrast possibilities even further. More-over, when there is opposition of an entire ensemble and the continuo alone, a valuable theatrical tool is created by the chiaroscuro in the orchestration.

Practicality is also at work here. In this period, which requires such a quantity of ornamentation from the soloist, composers have been wise to limit the accompaniment to continuo wherever the most improvisation is expected and desired. It is easily seen that at cadences this is almost always the case. A singer or violinist can risk the most elaborate ornaments when only one or two brains must collaborate with her; a full orchestra would make this too cumbersome and would limit her flexibility.

Imitating continuo requires a pianist to throw out everything he has learned about balance within his own part. The harpsichord cannot voice chords, so neither can the pianist-imitator. Singers performing continuo-accompanied arias or recitatives on the opera stage tell me that the bass line is really all they hear clearly. There is a subtle metallic "jingle" in the background, but the duet is clearly between soloist and the bass line, or in our case the soloist and our left hand. Skew the balance very, very significantly, favoring the bass line while muting the right hand. This approach will feel bizarre at first, but it is certain to give the impression of continuo—nothing else sounds quite like this in all our repertoire.

Remember too that ample, sensuous Steinway sounds have no place here. Avoid the damper pedal altogether if you can. It would be more stylistic to repeat a chord than to hold it with the pedal. Not only would this technique work against imitating the harpsichord, but the amount of sound would increase beyond what is possible for this period. If a bit more sound is required, add additional chord tones in the right hand. It is also stylistic—as it was with the harp—for the right hand's chords to be arpeggiated *ad libitum.*

EXAMPLE 8-38 Handel, "O sleep, why dost thou leave me?" *Semele*

This sublime aria is probably the softest, most personal moment in all of *Semele.* Remember that the left hand assumes the role of the solo cello, so the accompaniment, as is always the case with continuo, is very bottom-heavy. Do not, however, double the bass line an octave below, for double basses are not playing here. Even though the melody in the left hand outlines chords, the cello plays only one note at a time, crossing strings in the bargain, and a pianist must take care to preserve this articulation despite the temptation to think only in terms of the harmonic outlines, something idiomatic only for a pianist. Regardless of the edition, whatever the pianist is reading in his right hand is not by Handel. Do not feel obliged to limit what the right hand plays to what may be suggested by an editor.

EXAMPLE 8-39 Handel, "Or la tromba mi chiama a trionfar," *Rinaldo*

The preceding example was scored for continuo exclusively, and thus creates a rare and magical moment within any larger work. This aria, however, is typical of the vast majority of baroque pieces; measures for the full ensemble are juxtaposed with those for continuo only.

Some editions of reductions for piano will indicate the continuo areas with a distinctly different font or size of type, and these editions are wonderful time-savers for the busy collaborative pianist. If such a score is not available, the pianist needs to devise a method of marking the score so as to immediately indicate which force is playing. Simple brackets can do the job, and the choice of what they are indicating is up to the player—there are only two possibilities: tutti or continuo. The musical drama of the orchestra entering after a continuo section is enormous, and thus the pianist must separate these two sounds as much as possible. Here is a comparative chart as a reminder:

Orchestra	Continuo
Use the pedal	Minimal or no pedal
Notes struck together	Chords arpeggiated
Bass octave doubling	Cello only, no octaves
Normal balance	Significantly bottom-heavy
Full texture	Lean texture
Adapted for comfort	Seemingly improvised

EXAMPLE 8-40 Handel, "Frondi tenere," *Serse*

Fron - di te - ne - re   e bel - le   del mio pla - ta - no a - ma - to

A quick reminder here that a harpsichord is also playing within the orchestra, not only in solo moments. Thus when the orchestra's dynamic is low and pianistic conditions allow, the pianist-imitator can give us both elements simultaneously. The harpsichord's arpeggios are heard within the orchestra's synchronized chords.

EXAMPLE 8-41 Bach, "Mache dich, mein Herze, rein," *St. Matthew Passion*

Most performances of oratorios, passions, masses and motets take place in churches, and in these venues the harpsichord customarily used in operatic or

secular continuo work would be replaced by the organ, with or without an accompanying cello. It is not idiomatic for the organ to arpeggiate its chords, nor will the balance between the hands be as skewed toward the bass as we have seen in all the previous examples. The same "separateness" of continuo and full ensemble must be maintained, however, regardless of these other differences.

Almost a Conclusion

We have discussed all the instrumental colors to be imitated as well as a general philosophy about playing transcriptions and the importance of doing it enthusiastically and well. There still remain, however, many important concepts and prototypical situations to be considered before we can consider this aspect of collaboration complete. The next chapter continues this investigation into playing transcriptions and assumes that the techniques discussed above are understood and already part of the pianist's arsenal of tools.

NINE

More about Orchestral Playing

The Learning Process

Let us assume the homework on studying scores and listening to recordings has been done, the instrumentation has been marked on the pianist's music, and, as always, the words have been translated. Our imagination has been ignited, we know which sounds we are intent on imitating—the time has come to sit at the piano and learn the piece in question. I would suggest now that the process for learning something for orchestra differs significantly from that of learning something originally written for piano. With a keyboard accompaniment, we know from the outset that we must play our part—every note of it—as written. Each of us has a different way of learning a piece—perhaps hands practiced separately, perhaps very slowly, perhaps not, perhaps inserting dotted rhythms, perhaps avoiding pedal at the outset . . . whatever. The process is not at all dissimilar to that of learning a piece for solo piano.

With a transcription, using the same process will probably turn out to be an utter waste of time, for many of the notes on the transcribed page may not be playable; in other instances, accompaniments may need notes added. Things may change a great deal indeed. I believe it is imperative to begin one's learning of the transcribed material by playing the piece, section by section, *in the performance tempo* or very nearly so, with the sound of the orchestral version—the Document, remember?—always in our ears. Only then can the pianist discover what doesn't work with the transcription she is reading. Perhaps there are jumps too distant to be done safely in this tempo; perhaps certain notes do not last long enough; there may be a finger-busting passage of repeated pitches that could never be delivered comfortably. The possibilities—or should I say, impossibilities—are infinite. Only at the correct speed can these problems be detected. Since we are not able to replicate the letter of the law, and all changes are acceptable, why should a busy collaborator spend precious hours learning something she will be forced to change as soon as the performance tempo is introduced? *Make your initial decisions as close to tempo as possible.* What to play, what to add or subtract—mark these in your score (either writing or erasing), and only then proceed to learn the piece as you would a piece for piano. In other words: *the pianist revises the piece and then learns the revision.* No time is wasted; relative comfort and confidence are in place from the first moments of practice, and the final goal has been glimpsed before the learning begins. The pianist can now concentrate on capturing the essence of the music.

Making Changes

Various conditions can trigger the pianist's changing a published orchestral reduction:

- something is risky or downright impossible technically
- something is playable but does not capture the orchestral truth
- something is playable and sounds acceptable, but there is a better solution
- something is playable and sounds orchestral, but does not warrant my estimate of the many hours of practice required to master and guarantee it

With the first and last of these, a pianist must honor the voice in her head (and I know you hear it, pianists!) that warns: what you are about to practice will not work when you are nervous or dealing with an uncooperative instrument; or, this will always be semi-secure at best, never guaranteed; or, you will need hundreds of hours to learn this passage and few will even hear it or appreciate your pains. I have found that with utterly and obviously unplayable transcriptions, pianists are immediately aware of their need to revise things, and they behave accordingly. But I would emphasize the need to do this with each and every transcription we play, even slightly uncomfortable or risky moments in a score. Retain the legitimate challenges; I do not for a moment intend that we remove everything needing practice, but I do insist on things always feeling pianistically comfortable!

Before rewriting and substituting something of your own devising, it is important to identify the role of what you are about to revise. It might be melodic— something we would change very rarely; it might be something that sustains the piece; it might provide animation or rhythm. This is a completely subjective judgment, but a necessary one. Whatever the pianist then invents as a replacement needs to fill the same role. Perhaps tremolo can replace an alberti bass figure; repeated chords certainly could not. A trill might replace a pedal point octave tremolo quite successfully, but very playable scales could never be a proper substitute. If this principle of the Role Replacement is respected, all of the elements of the original are retained despite the revision. As you might guess, filling a role with an inappropriate or inadequate substitute can substantially change the character of a piece.

I should also acknowledge here and now that in selecting the following examples, I am advertising my own limitations and tarnishing what I hope is a decent reputation up to now. Many of you reading this text will not have any technical issues with many of the following examples, and I am envious in the extreme. At the same time, however, over a lifetime of playing and teaching I have found these to be problems common to more than just a few of us, so I happily acknowledge my own technical shortcomings if it will inspire others to be creative when transcriptions prove to be cantankerous.

Repeat, Please?

For the pianist, there is surely no greater pain in the neck than repeated-note figures. (Actually, our necks have nothing to do with it!) Every orchestral instrument, regardless of its family, can toss these off fairly easily through tonguing or bowing, whereas for a pianist, tension, discomfort, and fatigue can quickly enter the picture and immediately spoil any illusion of comfort. Various factors will contribute to a pianist's decision whether to find a practical fingering and drill it into the hand through practice or to rewrite the passage.

EXAMPLE 9-1 Rossini, "Una voce poco fa," *Il Barbiere di Siviglia*

This aria is inescapable for a collaborative pianist who works with voices, and these two measures, played three times, are some of the least pianistic in the piece. Up to a certain tempo, a pianist will feel secure with a clever fingering. (My own is notated in the example.) Even after hundreds of performances, however, the high F-sharps remain scary, the black keys being narrower and less forgiving than the white. Above a certain tempo, we need to consider changes. Assuming this passage needs rewriting, many editions suggest the following:

EXAMPLE 9-2 Rossini, "Una voce poco fa," *Il Barbiere di Siviglia*

Remembering that everything is subjective, I would state that I personally find this octave alternation adds a foreign, slurred element to a sassy figure. As I suggested earlier, we must respect the role of the figure we are replacing. The suggestion above respects the notion of replacing busy with busy, sixteenths with sixteenths, but I feel the clearly pianistic element of the slur distorts the orchestral original. For me, the role to be most mindful of is the brilliant, carefree, and crispy quality of the figure, not how many notes are played. If the tempo is too fast for me, I rewrite this passage in one of these two possible ways:

EXAMPLE 9-3, 9-4 Rossini, "Una voce poco fa," *Il Barbiere di Siviglia*

The tiny sixteenth-note rest affords me comfort, lightness, and sparkle. Could Rossini have written my revision? Could he approve what I'm about to practice and play? In this case, I would say: yes, most definitely.

EXAMPLE 9-5 Mozart, "Non so più, cosa son," *Le Nozze di Figaro*

Again tempo determines the practicality of this little figure, which occurs twice in this aria. Taken extremely fast, the repeated thirds can become too weighty or even unplayable. Not only is this music not in the brilliant area of the keyboard as was the Rossini example, but here Cherubino is singing in unison with the orchestra, further obscuring what we do at the piano. Assuming this needs to be rewritten, I can imagine two possibilities, both of which respect the role of busyness:

EXAMPLE 9-6, 9-7 Mozart, "Non so più cosa son," *Le Nozze di Figaro*

Of these two I much prefer the first choice. The richness of the orchestral thirds is preserved here, whereas in the second option the passagework not only sounds skimpy, but far worse, it risks sounding typical of keyboard music of the Classic period.

EXAMPLE 9-8 Verdi, "Cortigiani, vil razza," *Rigoletto*

The increased orchestral forces and heightened drama in mid-nineteenth-century operas pose ever-increasing challenges to the pianist who must cope with more complex figures. Here are two passages, immediately adjacent to each other, from the deformed jester's great aria. In the first, Verdi's accompaniment figure is easily played by the strings but is completely unpianistic. Since it is repeated for sixteen measures, it is an excellent investment of experimentation time to devise something practical and comfortable which still respects the original. The pianist's stamina must be carefully considered here when we are deciding what to play. We need to create an incisive, but not loud, eminently playable, comfortable figure. The repeated notes on the second and fourth beats are our nemesis. To remove sixteenth notes would take some acid out of this figure, as would inserting an octave alternation with a slur. Both would be relaxing for the pianist, but at too high a price for Rigoletto's anger. Here is one solution:

EXAMPLE 9-9 Verdi, "Cortigiani, vil razza," *Rigoletto*

By alternating the hands on beats two and four, the pianist avoids fatigue for the right hand, all the impulses are retained, and an inherently uncomfortable moment is turned into something tricky but far more comfortable. It still must be practiced carefully and probably memorized, but when this has been done, one can count on its succeeding, for it is now pianistic. My intention is never to make things unnecessarily easy, only to convert things into reasonable and practical challenges that get the job done.

The second example from the same aria is an easier challenge to meet. Although the piano score does not inform us properly, a quick listen tells us that there are twice as many impulses as we see. The tempo here is fast, making the repeated pitches impossible. A simple change to a rather familiar and idiomatic piano figure of alternating hands does the job nicely. It replaces busy with busy; no impulses are lost. Because it retains octaves in both hands for two measures, the fortissimo dynamic demanded by Verdi is easily provided:

EXAMPLE 9-10, 9-11 Verdi, "Cortigiani, vil razza," *Rigoletto*

Jumps

Repeated notes may win the prize for discomfort, but jumps are surely the first runner-up for this dubious crown. In the orchestra, the two elements, bottom and top, making up a jump may be played by different instruments—thus there is no jump really, or the interval that is problematic for the pianist is accomplished with the press of a button or the change of a string only small fractions of an inch away. For us at the keyboard, however, intervals equal space, often requiring a change in hand position or, at the very least, an attenuated stretch. Do this at a fast enough tempo and/or steadily over a significant period of time and, to quote the Apollo 13 astronauts: "Houston, we have a problem." As I have been emphasizing continually: such difficulties have no place in playing orchestral music on the piano; any illusion we might hope to create is lost to the sounds of labor and risk.

EXAMPLE 9-12, 9-13 Donizetti, "O luce di quest'anima," *Linda di Chamounix*

EXAMPLE 9-12, 9-13 Continued

O lu -ce di quest' a - ni - ma   de - li - zia a - mor - e   vi – ta

First, play the measures accompanying the singer's first entrance in this cabaletta (measures 10–14). Note how easy, light, and breezy the soprano's support system sounds and feels. Now return to the eight-measure introduction. What felt comfortable with two hands must now be accomplished with only one, but the leggiero character of these alternating chords must remain as before. Add octaves to the bass notes to increase the orchestral impression, and the problem intensifies. Now we are executing large hand position shifts far too quickly for comfort and grace. Even memorized and benefiting from Donizetti's choice of an all-white key, this can now sound like a Valkyrie in full war cry if we are not vigilant. All we need do is reduce the space between the top and bottom notes of the jump and the problem is considerably alleviated. Does it really matter how high the top chord is or how it is voiced? Or, if the register and inversion of the top chord is assigned a high priority, perhaps the added octaves might be sacrificed without guilt. This introduction is playable as printed, but the identical atmosphere can be created without worry by reducing the span of the jump.

EXAMPLE 9-14, 9-15　Tchaikovsky, "Tatiana's letter scene," *Eugene Onegin*

Here is a similar example, but with faster, less audible jumps for the left hand. Measures and measures of this accompanimental pattern confront the pianist. The orchestra is large, the right hand too must cover a great deal of space (unlike in the previous example) and must imitate diverse instruments as well. The panting nature of the off-beats in the left hand is the role to be retained, not the actual spelling of the syncopated chords that create it. The Donizetti example was staccato and thus quite naked, but here the pedal is down for longer periods of time, further masking which chords we are playing on the upper end of the jumps in the left hand. Move these extremes closer together, and a smoothness is easily achieved, aiding and abetting the right hand's melodic contribution.

EXAMPLE 9-16, 9-17 Verdi, "Tacea la notte placida," *Il Trovatore*

Di ta - le a-mor, che dir — — si   mal può dal-la pa-

ro — — - la,   d'a-mor   che in-ten-do io

Allegro giusto

In the cabaletta to Leonora's opening aria, the voice is treated instrumentally, and singer and orchestra together become an etude in giddy staccato leaps. In the orchestra the tasks are easy ones, and again, no jumps hamper the steadiness of the eighth notes. Bringing the left-hand notes closer together provides a rock-solid basis for it all. In the right hand, omitting a note is far preferable to being even minimally late because of an awkward jump. Keyboard geography must not play a role in our work here or anywhere with transcriptions.

EXAMPLE 9-18, 9-19 Saint-Saëns, "Mon coeur s'ouvre à ta voix," *Samson et Dalila*

This is one of the French repertoire's loveliest arias, but on the piano the first verse is extremely difficult to execute for a number of reasons: while *both* hands must jump an octave without the time to feel pianistically comfortable, the strings are divided in such a fashion so that each player plays only one beat's worth of music. Therefore in reality no jumps exist; there are no terrors for the orchestra. And did I mention that we are in a black-note key, automatically giving the feeling of walking with insecure footing? The cherry on this unwanted sundae is the pianissimo dynamic. We must find something comfortable or Samson is certain to decline Dalila's offer of a haircut.

My own solution involves dividing the chords differently between the hands, thus gaining the ability to negotiate the jump safely with a subtle slur. It is not possible to do this in every measure, but it can be done with the opening and enough bars following to create a serene texture under the mezzo's cantilena and for the pianist to emerge relatively unscathed, perhaps even poetic.

Double Your Trouble

Here is an example of a passage in an aria where *both* jumps and repeated notes must be dealt with simultaneously. As always, we must find a practical and comfortable solution which can be guaranteed.

EXAMPLE 9-20, 9-21 Verdi, "E sogno o realtà?" *Falstaff*

EXAMPLE 9-20, 9-21 Continued

For the first three measures, the right hand can use a traditional fingering for the repeated G-flats. If the octave change in the third bar causes a mishap or needs extra time, leaving out the first high note will easily rectify this problem. The left hand, however, cannot execute the triplet on the first beat *and* jump to the higher octave with any sense of security or steady rhythmic pulse. My solution is to omit the third triplet note, and do so three times successively. To include the entire triplet in the fourth bar—simply because it is possible—would advertise the simplification of the previous two bars and ruin Verdi's ostinato pattern.

Bars 4 through 7 are playable for some pianists, but not so easily for many of us. I retain the two-note slurred figure but omit the third note of each beat so I can survive to the end of the passage. Again, doing things consistently many times in a row, even if not absolutely necessary, can confirm the impression that the composer could have written the pattern as we have revised it.

Pruning Passagework

Many orchestral instruments execute fast passagework with more agility and less labor than we poor keyboard animals can. Stamina and fatigue may also enter the picture if these busy measures continue long enough. If a pianist feels unevenness or heaviness setting in, I see no reason why a note here or there cannot be omitted. (I suggested this earlier with "Una voce poco fa.") I caution not to use this idea indiscriminately or too often. It should be used only when truly necessary, and it should never turn busy accompaniments into serene ones simply to avoid practicing difficult passagework.

EXAMPLE 9-22, 9-23 Massenet, "Letter scene," *Werther*

Werther's second letter to his beloved speaks of the happy noise of children outside his window; all is frivolous, young, light as a feather. The septuplets here pose no problem for the violins. On the keyboard, however, this is very fast, feels awkward, and can easily add years onto the age of each child, to say nothing of the pianist herself! In addition, the mezzo-soprano will be grateful if she can clearly detect the first note of each group, both pitch and rhythm. All of this is made possible with five-note figurations rather than seven, and to my ear, the sparkle and busyness remain absolutely in place. We can play this revision for hours and actually enjoy it—not so the original.

Cholesterol Territory

In the previous chapter, in discussing string tremolo I introduced the notion that the middle register of the piano was the most useful for hiding things, adding behind-the-scenes filler without attracting undue attention. This can, of course, hold true whether or not tremolo is involved. The nearer one is to middle-C, the more generic and beautifully all-purpose the sound becomes. Adding "meat" or "bulk" too low on the keyboard risks a dramatic low brass implication; add things too high, and stridency can develop. The middle of the keyboard is perfect for these needs.

EXAMPLE 9-24, 9-25 Gounod, "Ah, lève-toi, soleil," *Roméo et Juliette*

EXAMPLE 9-24, 9-25 Continued

In the reprise of the opening theme of this aria, the violins double the tenor's melody, thus occupying the right hand entirely. We need the depth of lower octaves in the left hand to support these higher voices and to ennoble Romeo's second utterance of these gorgeous words. Without the introducing of "stuffing" after each downbeat, these extremes would lack adequate support. Remember: these tremolos really begin on the downbeats in the orchestra; make the audience believe they were there all the time by introducing them as surreptitiously as possible.

EXAMPLE 9-26, 9-27 Strauss, "Sein wir wieder gut," *Ariadne auf Naxos*

EXAMPLE 9-26, 9-27 Continued

EXAMPLE 9-26, 9-27 Continued

With the words "Die Welt ist lieblich, und nicht fürchterlich dem Mutigen" ("The world is lovely and not frightening to the brave"), Strauss gives his hero very high-lying melodies, doubled in the orchestra, and underpinned with deep bass notes. The right hand is transcribed (perhaps by Strauss himself?) with running triplets, which certainly add activity to keep things going, but I do not find these sufficient to support both bass and treble. I add cholesterol in the middle of the piano, in the middle of each new harmony, with just a bit of tremolo with my left hand. At the same time I incorporate the triplets into block chords rather than octaves in the right hand's tune. The texture is now equalized from top to bottom, the singer feels well supported, and, I hope I sound more like the Document.

Busy for Busy

Once a role of a passage has been identified as providing the animation, the urgency, the heat of a piece, we must decide whether to learn it as it is or to rewrite it. Omitting it is not an option; we need fast notes. Tremolo would be easy, but it does not provide the sweeping range of the original and might be far too generic. And yet, it is clear that a great deal of time would be required to master the notes as the composer wrote them. With orchestral reductions we must always balance learning time against effect provided. In many cases, *anything* busy of a scalar nature will provide the identical effect; the role of the troublesome passage is filled, and the pianist has time for other problems.

Two other factors may enter the decision-making process for the pianist. First, is the soloist performing during the passage in question? If so, the spotlight is shared and the camouflage is easier to achieve. If not, there may no way to avoid learning the pesky original. Second, in which period of music is this piece found, and what is the harmonic rhythm during this event? If we are speaking of Mozart, little can be hidden, and even pedaling will not remove one's naked feeling. If, on the other hand, the piece is romantic or impressionistic, the use of the pedal will probably be permissive and generous. We can tuck our rewritten passagework into larger envelopes of sound and harmony without worrying.

EXAMPLE 9-28, 9-29 Wagner, "Du bist der Lenz," *Die Walküre*

EXAMPLE 9-28, 9-29 Continued

This might be called a vocal explosion rather than an aria, for Sieglinde's feelings burst out of her after she hears her brother's impassioned aria immediately preceding. Only eight measures are calm, while all the rest are filled with quick crescendi, sudden pianos, sweeping and wide-ranging passagework for the orchestra. Wagner's chromaticism, used liberally here, makes for unfamiliar and tricky, uncomfortable patterns for the hand and could easily qualify as etude-level writing for the piano. Even the violins complain about this writing.

I see no reason to spend the time necessary to master these intricate passages. Once the harmonies are identified, notated with symbols if necessary, it is a simple matter to execute *familiar* scale patterns at this fast speed. Take care not to exceed the highest note in the original. To play enough notes, it may be necessary to execute more ups and downs, or perhaps double back or turn around so as to finish where an ending is required. The soprano is singing expressively during this entire rhapsodic event, and she feels the same billowing, breezy, fantastic patterns underneath her as she would with the original. The audience revises its opinion that Wagner is impossible on the piano, and everyone is happy—no one more so than the pianist!

Incidentally, the very last measure of this section must be played as printed, for the singer is now silent, the storm is abating, and we need this bridge into the calmer, more retrospective section at hand. No rewriting here—take all the time you did *not* spend practicing the previous bars and learn this one.

EXAMPLE 9-30 Mozart, "Batti, batti," *Don Giovanni*

Just for comparison's sake, consider the first three measures of the allegretto section of this aria. This is a rather unusual orchestration for Mozart; it features a cello obligato, hence the scales for the left hand. This music is not chromatic; the classic period obviously demands clean, very stingy pedaling. We have no choice but to practice this annoyingly difficult passage and play it as written. (I must admit to often playing the first three measures with my hands crossed. I'm not proud of my need to do so, but I *am* usually pleased with the result.)

EXAMPLE 9-31, 9-32 Verdi, "Condotta egl'era in ceppi," *Il Trovatore*

EXAMPLE 9-33, 9-34 Verdi, "Pace, pace, mio Dio," *La Forza del destino*

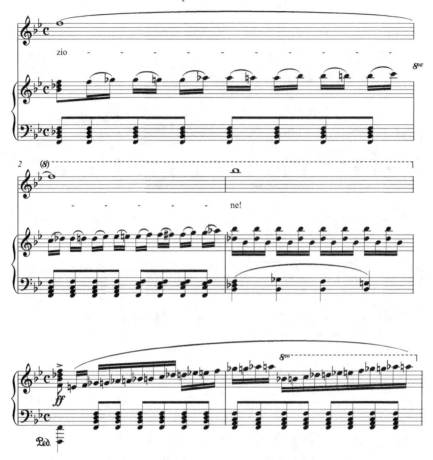

Here are two climactic moments for mezzo-soprano and soprano respectively which involve the whole orchestra at a high dynamic. There is no way a transcription for piano could include everything that is actually happening. Two roles are being performed simultaneously by the orchestra: the winds and brass are playing sustained harmonies while the strings provide the animation *inside* these harmonic envelopes, outlining diminished chords in the *Trovatore* example and climbing chromatically in *Forza*. So far, so good—everything is playable. But the technical plot thickens because both these string figurations involve repeated pitches at very fast speeds—a picnic for the strings, and a nightmare for the pianist. Standing on the opera stage, the singers in both these arias hear the long sustained chords, but only *feel* the busy passagework.

Let us replace busy with busy. Sweeping diminished-seventh chord arpeggios, both up and down, with *no repeated notes* work perfectly for the first example. For the second, determine the ending pitch which must be reached at the end of the ascending chromatic scale; count downward the number of *non-repeated* sixteenth-notes necessary to reach this pitch, and *voilà!*, you determine your starting pitch. A chromatic scale is familiar and comfortable . . . that is, when repeated notes are not involved! The electricity and brilliance of the rising strings is retained, the singer feels a dramatic force underneath her, all at surprisingly small cost for the pianist. We are not playing fewer notes than the orchestra plays, but ours are pianistic. Generous pedaling masks this clever handiwork and gives the impression of the sustained brass and woodwind chords.

Adding to Subtract

Occasionally it is difficult to imitate the orchestra because the piano part has too *few* notes. When this is the case, the ear can hear each note too clearly and distinctly rather than the "wash" effect provided by the original. If the role to be filled is a background, all-purpose sweep, we need enough notes to achieve this at the piano.

EXAMPLE 9-35 Bizet, "Je dis que rien ne m'épouvante," *Carmen*

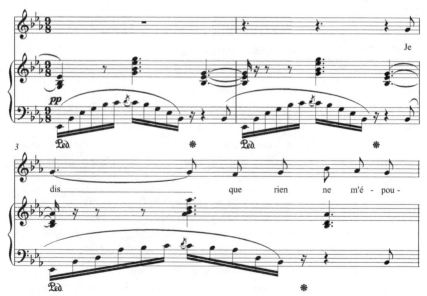

EXAMPLE 9-36, 9-37 Puccini, "Che gelida manina," *La Bohème*

Compare these two left-hand accompaniments. Whether or not the traditional speed of the *Carmen* aria is just a bit faster than the *Bohème* excerpt, the moving notes in the left hand draw attention to themselves as both harmonic outlines and give a slight melodic inference at their highest point. Thus I know no acceptable way to avoid playing the printed original. With the arpeggios by Puccini, the tempo is broader, there is no melodic component to the left hand, and thus the details are heard far too much. The reduction is not incorrect; it simply does not translate well to the keyboard. I add fast (and easy) arpeggios, retaining the correct bass notes only on beats one and three. This makes me sound orchestral, and coincidentally gives me the ability to sound confident and secure—exactly what I want to offer my tenor as he pauses to pray and prepare for his famous high C.

Fortepianos for Pianofortes

With thirty-two sonatas' worth of *fp*'s, orchestral music requiring this effect should pose no difficulty for pianists. And yet this quick dynamic sting and re-treat is used so differently in the orchestra's contribution to opera and concerti that it needs a moment's attention here. In works for piano, if a *fp* is followed im-mediately by more music, we simply play one loud impulse and change to soft with the next impulse; if the requested *fp* is the last note in a phrase, all we can do is allow the natural decay of our instrument to create the effect, but the dramatic suddenness is definitely compromised.

With repertoire for orchestra, we often find this effect in accompanied recita-tive or recitative-like events within larger sections, both highly dramatic moments. Mozart's operas are particularly rich in these devices. It is inevitably theatrical, usually played by the strings, serving as a kind of fanfare for an important com-ment from the singer or concerto soloist. It also serves to get the orchestra out of the soloist's way so that important information can be imparted without undue competition from the accompaniment. With the tiniest flick of the bow, this sud-den change in dynamics can be achieved, far faster than the decay on any modern piano. It would be a shame to lose this dramatic tool.

I have heard pianists attempt to imitate this effect by leaving the keys after striking a chord and quickly grabbing the resonance with the pedal. When this technique works, it is very successful, but when it fails (and it does far too often), it leaves both performers with an embarrassed silence on their hands. This is far too risky and insecure a solution for my taste. My method of imitating an or-chestral *fp* chord simply amounts to striking a chord loudly and then quickly re-leasing *some* of its notes so as to leave fewer notes to resonate. The pedal comes down *after* this release so only the reduced version of the chord is captured and held. The remaining chord must, of course, be complete. If there are not adequate notes in the initial chord to allow removing some and still retaining all the neces-sary chord tones, then the pianist must add notes to the chord's initial impact, expressly for the purpose of removing them.

EXAMPLE 9-38, 9-39, 9-40, 9-41 Mozart, "Come scoglio," *Così fan tutte*

As Fiordiligi shows her "Albanian" visitors the door, her recitative is particularly imperious and benefits immensely from a liberal use of these fortepianos. I have tried to show the notes to be removed and retained to create this effect. Note that the bass note to be retained may be the high or low octave, depending on the performers' wishes.

EXAMPLE 9-42, 9-43 Massenet, "Je marche sur tous les chemins," *Manon*

Je mar-che sur tous les che - mins

Mes che-vaux cou- rent à grands pas

De-vant ma vie a - ven-tu- reu - se

EXAMPLE 9-42, 9-43 Continued

Each of Manon's impertinent phrases is ignited by a *fp* chord in the strings. The piano transcription does not always begin with enough depth to create enough effect. Adding low bass notes expressly in order to remove them does the trick. Compare this section with the minor chords in the second strophe, where no changes are needed because there is adequate depth initially.

Where's That Tune?

This subject really confounds and irritates me. I cannot, for the life of me, understand how crucial melodic events, uttered by the orchestra, by other singers, or by both can have been omitted from the transcriber's version for piano. I have said often enough in this chapter that everything is subjective, that one person's priorities may be vastly different from another's in a choice of what to play, but here I am speaking of melodies no less important than the soloist's. I cannot begin to conceive of doing without them.

I am also concerned that no soloist ever be confronted with anything at an orchestral rehearsal that surprises and therefore distracts her, ruining her concentration and musical plans. This point is particularly crucial when the pianist is partnering younger, less experienced artists who have not yet performed the piece with orchestra or in a complete production with other singers. At the piano we owe soloist, audience, and ourselves the most complete, convincing experience we can muster.

EXAMPLE 9-44, 9-45 Puccini, "Quando m'en vo," *La Boheme*

EXAMPLE 9-44, 9-45 Continued

Two other singers share moments with Musetta in her famous waltz-song. In the case of Alcindoro, her escort for the evening, I find that the most recent anthologies of arias do indeed insert his two solo interjections into the pianist's lines. These are necessary for filling the silent beats of their bars even if they offer scant melodic gifts to Musetta, who does not really care about him anyway. However, the missing melody I speak of here is in the tune's reprise, when Mimì gives her opinion of the situation. Her first lines are doubled in the orchestra and therefore printed for the pianist, but to omit her soaring phrase a bit later seems a crime to me. Worse, it deprives us of the "dueling sopranos" effect; Musetta's high B will sound more glorious when it trumps Mimì's high A heard only a measure before.

EXAMPLE 9-46, 9-47 Verdi, "Sul fil d'un soffio etesio," *Falstaff*

germo - gli-no pa - ro - - le.

Pa - ro - le al-lu - mi - na - te

EXAMPLE 9-46, 9-47 Continued

This is the briefest moment imaginable in the second strophe of this ecstatic aria, but in terms of color, this is a masterstroke of the composer's pen. Extremely high harmonics in the violins triple the magic in the atmosphere here; Disney could not have imagined a more fairy-princess sound. Any Nanetta hearing this addition to her singing for the first time will feel herself transported, as do we. This is so simple for any pianist to add, taking all the sextuplets in the left hand, and, without it, these measures are so plain. Why is this tune never printed in piano scores?

EXAMPLE 9-48, 9-49 Saint-Saëns, "Mon coeur s'ouvre à ta voix," *Samson et Dalila*

EXAMPLE 9-48, 9-49 Continued

This is one of the most glaring (and daring) omissions in all of opera, and there is no justifiable excuse for it. Whether it be the complete piano score of the opera or any one of the available anthologies of arias, the published accompaniment to this second refrain sends a false message—or rather, *no* message—to singer and audience alike.

First of all, Dalila's voluptuous melody is now doubled by the violins, whereas in the first refrain she was alone with harp only. This accompaniment would have a tangible effect on how any mezzo-soprano would sing; she has more competition and less freedom than before. Then in the third measure, the tenor, no longer unaffected by her entreaties, begins to sing and with him the entire wind section too. Thus all the musical forces are in duet mode, the two melodies sensuously interweaving and spurring each other on. What does the pianist see? Only the most minimal of accompaniments instead of the antiphonal symphony this aria has now become. A pianist, doing her utmost to recreate this extravagant texture, will not be able to finish any of the phrases—string or wind—without neglecting the beginning of another. But no matter . . . the listener's ear will gladly finish the various lines.

Three Is Definitely a Crowd

Even the most resourceful and inventive pianist, someone with significant experience with transcriptions, will find herself challenged by moments when three elements are at work in the orchestral fabric simultaneously. Managing the imitation of individual instrumental colors, creating sustained, rich sounds, turning awkward events into comfortable ones—these are all possible and clearly within reach for an open-minded, imaginative, and informed pianist, as we have seen. Dividing the jobs between the hands, or asking one hand to multi-task—to play arco and pizzicato simultaneously, for example—we are still in the realm of the possible, if also the more demanding. Add a third element, with space required between the registers to involve nearly the entire keyboard, and one begins to wonder: How on earth am I to handle this? Should one avoid performing this piece with piano altogether?

The motivated collaborator answers with a resounding, enthusiastic "No!" and sets about summoning all her creativity to negotiate this complex, triple-task situation. If anything, the extra challenge feeds her sense of adventure. She senses too that when these "impossible" moments have been converted to difficult but pianistic events, she will probably be as proud of her handiwork as she has ever been of anything. It will be well worth her time and trouble. There is no universal formula for playing transcriptions, and particularly not with this puzzle of three simultaneous elements. The pianist must either simplify whichever she considers the least important of the three, or revise an important element which she feels can most easily wear a disguise. Here are some examples from the standard operatic repertoire.

EXAMPLE 9-50, 9-51 Leoncavallo, "Ballatella," *I Pagliacci*

EXAMPLE 9-50, 9-51 Continued

EXAMPLE 9-50, 9-51 Continued

The entire 28-measure reprise of Nedda's opening tune is sensuously accompanied, now with the very welcome added element of the cellos doubling the vocal line. The right hand is sadly unavailable for assisting here; it is in the stratosphere with a busy and all too detectable pattern which provides the rhythmic motor for the whole aria. This obviously leaves the left hand with the two tasks of bass line and melody. All the editions of this piece for piano divide the duties identically but unacceptably. Many problems ensue with the left hand doing everything:

- The bass line is sometimes raised an octave so as to be reachable while one is playing the cello tune, but not consistently. As the music climbs and grows, doing this becomes increasingly problematic for a rich, orchestral sound and a soprano singing generously above. The skyscraper needs a basement.
- The bass notes that remain unreachable are notated as grace-notes; we have already covered this taboo in these pages and I cannot relent even for this complex texture. These are not idiomatic for any orchestra.
- Strategic bass notes are totally omitted from the score, thus changing the larger harmonic picture quite significantly, and now and then turning the tune into the bass line as if this were a Baroque aria.

We can and must improve on things.

- Play all the bass notes well below the tune, *always* on the beat, *never* as grace notes.
- Add the missing bass pitches to measures 5, 7, 9, 11, and 13.

This leaves us with the principal tune, which, rather surprisingly, is the element to be simplified in this instance. This compromise is easily hidden, since the singer is supplying the missing melodic pitches. If this is done with alacrity, the listener will never know that the cellos have omitted *fourteen* beautiful, cantabile impulses.

EXAMPLE 9-52, 9-53 Puccini, "Recondita armonia," *Tosca*

EXAMPLE 9-52, 9-53 Continued

The four-bar reprise of Cavaradossi's opening melody has problems similar but not quite identical to those in the previous example. Instead of a moving bass line, we have a stationary dominant pedal point here. As the harmonies above vacillate, bass notes will have to be re-articulated and the pedal will require changing every measure to avoid losing the bass or serving up tonic and dominant harmonies in the same pedal, neither of which is acceptable.

Puccini's melody is heard in octaves above and below middle C, a very different task from Leoncavallo's tune in single notes only. It is quickly discovered that both hands are needed for the two elements of bass line and melody to sound at once. Nor can we cleverly omit melodic notes, for the tenor is not doubling the initial bars of tune here. He is, in fact, a fourth element.

I believe the solution rests with the shimmering tremolo, heard high in the strings. Whereas with Nedda's aria the right-hand figurations were too obvious to be altered, here the tremolo is our salvation, for it has no inherent rhythmic implications and is probably the least precise of any accompanimental device we might encounter. Try omitting the tremolo on the four downbeats in question, using the right hand for the first melodic note in each bar. Then begin the tremolo as subtly and stealthily as you can; the goal is to make the listener believe it had been there all along. Done cleverly enough, and with a passionate tenor partner singing his heart out, the illusion will succeed and all three elements will pass muster.

EXAMPLE 9-54, 9-55 Strauss, "Sein wir wieder gut," *Ariadne auf Naxos*

Wagner and Strauss consistently present the thorniest transcription problems for a pianist, but fortunately for us, few of their arias are excerptable or frequently performed out of context, though this one is becoming almost standard fare nowadays, particularly for auditions when an aria in German is required. For me, Strauss is usually the more challenging of the two composers, for in addition to the predilection for harmonic and sonic richness which they share, Strauss inevitably adds audible contrapuntal lines to the texture. This pattern is nowhere more evident than in *Ariadne*, where a chamber orchestra is in the pit.

These four measures near the end of this exuberant monolog are another example of three elements sounding at once with significant separation of their registers. Neither hand can play two elements completely. The right hand is fully occupied with the jaunty leitmotif (in octaves!) heard ever since the opera began, and it certainly cannot handle any additional music. The left hand will have to be responsible for all the bass notes—always essential—and the hyperactive mid-range counterpoint. The tempo is quite fast, making the jumps in the left hand problematic. If this were an artsong ("Cäcilie" or "Nichts!" for example), we could take a bit of time when it was needed, rubato being always part and parcel of the Strauss style. For orchestra, as was previously discussed, this solution is inappropriate and, worse, it would accustom the singer to an accompaniment and an accommodation she will never hear in the opera house. The middle-voice tunes can be played, but only in truncated versions so that jumps in both directions can be done confidently, accurately, with no distortion of the rhythm. Since every other bar features identical material in sequences, be sure to similarly duplicate your choices as you decide what to play; anything played twice is automatically more convincing.

Coda

After all the listening, rewriting, considering how a revision sounds, and weighing the probability of technical success in a pressurized performance situation, there is yet one important question to ask yourself before you ink in what you intend to play: "Could the composer have written this?" An affirmative answer is required before your decisions can be finalized. Some questions that might cast doubts are the following:

- Octave doubling in the bass
  Have I introduced this at the right time? Have I stopped the doubling appropriately?
- Added missing melodies
  Have I accounted for how this additional tune begins and ends? Have I braided the new tune into the existing transcription musically?
- Depth and height
  Have I exceeded what is stylistic for this period?
- Filler devices
  Have I chosen something (tremolo or syncopated chords, e.g.) that is anachronistic for this composer? Have I chosen something that oversteps the filler role and sounds too prominent or too interesting?

Hopefully, your revisions have been carefully and expertly calculated, and you can now bring the gavel down proudly on your own version of this orchestral piece. You have notated all this information in your personal shorthand that perhaps no one else would understand but in markings that tell you everything *you* need to know. Now make a photocopy, as you would with your passport prior to traveling abroad. This revised transcription is extremely valuable; it represents a great deal of your time; it has been sampled, tested, re-revised, re-sampled, and approved; it is custom tailored to your technique and speaks to your own priorities. For myself, I'd rather misplace my wallet than lose one of my rewritten orchestral transcriptions!

Finally let me say that these two chapters devoted to orchestral accompaniment are together the longest section with the most detailed information in this text, and it would be easy for the novice pianist-imitator to feel overwhelmed. That is not my intention, although I know there is much to digest and hours of experimentation ahead. I can only promise you that the more pieces you prepare with these principles in mind, the easier it all becomes. Less and less will need to be written down; your instructions to yourself will become more economical and more specific; your arsenal of devices, tricks, and comfortable changes which capture the orchestration and can still be guaranteed will grow and grow. You will look back at reductions you learned earlier before encountering these suggestions and be amused (or appalled) at how you may have struggled unwisely or perhaps didn't struggle enough. You will begin to look forward to preparing your next transcription and receiving the inevitable compliment: "Wow! You sound like an orchestra!" You will deserve it.

TEN

Odds and Ends

Most of the miscellany in this chapter are mechanical, technical, or procedural issues, but that is not at all to suggest that they are insignificant. Quite the opposite, actually. Paying attention to such details cannot make a performance excellent, but ignoring them or adopting a careless or casual attitude about them can certainly spoil the experience for everyone.

Before and After

This is a particular passion of mine. No matter how beautifully a pianist may collaborate while playing, creating perfect ensemble, inflecting identically to the singer, structuring and scripting introductions, interludes, and postludes so it seems as if the soloist's mind is playing the piano—all of this can be undermined if care is not taken with the moments immediately before and after a piece. This requires being visually in touch with one's partner at all times.

There are several ways a piece might begin. Sometimes with a very direct or animated song, something humorous or angry, the singer may decide to flip a switch and *become* the song in an instant. It is imperative that the collaborative pianist be ready in advance, tempo in his mind, position on the keys, "pre-hearing" the music. He sees the singer's sharp change, and presto! . . . his own preparation allows him to mirror that change, and the music begins. If the singer takes longer than expected to begin, and the pianist finds he has extra time with the music playing in his head, no matter. *Not* being ready would be the problem; the singer would feel silly to be exhibiting a mood and have no audible support.

Sometimes a singer may elect to have the pianist draw her into the song; this is often the case with long introductions. Again, by being aware of the singer's subtle shift from neutral to ready-to-be-invited, the pianist can safely begin, letting the singer use the introduction for her preparation, timing her first sung notes perfectly. This is a subtler visual cue or perhaps even none at all, but with experimentation and enough experience with a specific partner, this aspect of collaboration can provide the perfect frosting on the cake. The pianist can discuss a plan for beginning this or that with his partner, but on stage, of course, anything can happen, and plans are constantly in flux. There truly is no substitute for consistently keeping one's partner on the radar screen if these beautiful beginnings are to be achieved. Don't stare at your partner; nothing looks worse than a pianist resembling a puppy waiting for a treat. Rather, expand the circle of your relaxed vision to include your partner, and you will have everything you need.

Conversely, how we behave at the conclusion of a song can mar the most expressive atmosphere irreparably. The audience should see twins on stage, one seated, the other standing in the curve of the piano. If a piece ends with a flourish, a slap, or a joke, and the singer chooses a sharp, clean exit from the mood, then obviously the pianist's remaining involved would look absurd. In more sensitive endings, there is often a slow and gradual dissolution of the mood during the last note or even afterward, and the pianist must do nothing physically to hasten or make this process abrupt. One of the problems is the fact that the last note a pianist plays can be held with the pedal and doesn't really require our physical participation on the keyboard itself. But nothing looks less collaborative than a pianist carelessly leaving the keys, dropping his hands in his lap, and depending on his foot alone to prolong the expression while his partner is still experiencing the music's afterglow. Even after the last keyboard note is released, there is more to be experienced. This silent music is to be savored and matched to the soloist's gradual withdrawal from the mood. One can see intensity in a pianist's body, his arms, his head, his eyes, whether or not there is still sound to be heard. When I see the singer still involved in a song while the pianist has removed his hands cavalierly from the keyboard—or worse, has begun to turn to the next song!—I know this pianist has no aptitude for collaboration.

Who's Got That Pitch?

In chapter 6 I made very brief mention of the need to give an emergency pitch, should the singer's plan to find it on her own fail. Let me elaborate here on the whole subject of giving pitches. In rehearsal it will be determined whether it is prudent to give the singer the responsibility of finding the next opening pitch when there is no introduction to assist her. Various methods of securing the note can be suggested by the pianist, but sometimes the interval needed proves too difficult, and success does not feel guaranteed. This situation is not ideal, but neither is it the end of the world; I would rather worry about so many other issues.

The pianist should cheerfully volunteer to give the pitch and not make his partner feel inept,stupid, or lacking in musicianship. Nevertheless the composer's intention to surprise the listener should also be retained as much as possible. I never give a harmonized pitch, for the audience would then know the key of the piece. I also give the single note in a different octave from where it will be sung. This device protects the spontaneity of the opening too, for the audience cannot intuit where in the singer's range she will begin. Needless to say, I give this note clearly but also as quietly as I can.

When a pitch is needed for the first piece in a set, some variations are possible. The pianist can make a point of calculating the pitch needed from the end of the previous set, and then sing it to his partner backstage. Doing so requires a bit of trust between the two as well as good musicianship from our friend at the keyboard, the pianist. Pitchpipes can also be brought backstage by either performer, further simplifying things. Finally, if the pianist walks quickly enough to the keyboard, and the applause is sufficiently enthusiastic (isn't it always?), the note can be struck a bit louder than *pp* andeven in the *correct* octave, and still remain inaudible to the audience. I have done this innumerable times, and not once has it been mentioned by anyone afterwards.

Turning Over a New Leaf

This is a very personal issue, and probably no two collaborative pianists share the same philosophy about it. For myself, I will go to any lengths to avoid a page turner when I am accompanying a singer. I have turned several measures earlier than the end of a page as well as after many measures of the next page have elapsed throughout my career. With Debussy's "Chevaux de bois" I begin with page 7 in front of me and play pages 1 through 6 by heart. I don't expect praise or admiration for this. If I choose to do this it is because I feel that with vocal recitals the moods being created are so often more personal, more fragile, more vulnerable than is the case with an instrumental sonata. The singer is always performing from memory—unlike a violinist or clarinetist—and thus there is the potential of a very palpable, visual connection between the audience and the artist on stage. For me, nothing spoils this special atmosphere more than an extraneous figure popping up and down, worrying, rising, reaching, clearly hoping not to make a mistake, and all too often doing so anyway.

With an instrumental partner, I feel less passionate about all of this. I mean no disrespect—I really love performing with these folks too—but the fact is, there are mechanics between performer and audience that do not exist with a singer. There is also often a music stand and a score. There is no poetry, at least the verbal kind. All of this allows me to feel less guilty adding a third party to what's happening on stage. With sonatas and larger chamber works there are usually much fiercer and more constant technical demands for the pianist. During the Kreutzer sonata, for example, it is all I can manage just to execute the piano part; turning my own pages or memorizing such a quantity of music is more than I feel obliged to handle.

Even with instrumental repertoire, however, I will ask the person at my left to turn only if doing so is really necessary. If I have enough time to turn gracefully on my own, I will write "No" at the end of the page to indicate I will turn it myself. At the end of each movement I do the same to save embarrassment all around.

Let me finish this bothersome, unmusical subject by saying that at no time would I want to be uncomfortable—musically, technically, or emotionally—because of using or not using a page turner. Performing is difficult enough; let your choices about pages make you more comfortable, not less.

What Was That Tempo?

If a pianist plays beautifully, synchronizes his notes with every word, maintains perfect balance, and yet consistently miscalculates the basic tempo of a piece, he will not find himself fielding too many requests for his services. An ability to recall the rehearsed and agreed-upon tempo is crucial for the collaborator.

The fact that an accompaniment is full of notes does not guarantee that it is the best guide for remembering a tempo. As we practice on our own, the tempo may fluctuate rather significantly since we are naturally concentrating on the pianism and virtuosity required. Therefore I would usually recommend using the music of one's partner for the purpose of imprinting a tempo. If it is a vocal piece, text plays an enormous role in selecting the perfect speed. Prove this to yourself: Choose a coloratura passage in a Rossini aria and sing it without words, monitoring your speed; now repeat it with the Italian text—it will probably be a trifle more controlled in tempo; now find a Peters edition and sing the same run in German translation—what has happened to the tempo now? The encroachment of consonants definitely slows things down. In addition to words, there may be awkward jumps in the vocal line or tricky melismas to consider. In seeking to imprint a tempo in your brain, find the busiest moment in every sense, identify it as your tempo guide, and in rehearsal pay particular attention to the sound of the soloist during this event. Later, seated quietly at the piano, hear the selected passage again; re-experience it wholly: the diction and the singer's progress from note to note.

This event may be buried deep in the middle of the piece, but the pianist needs to retrieve its imprint before beginning. In a performance, the retrieval of the event from our inner memory must begin quite soon after the previous song has concluded in order for us to hear it and refine it as many times as possible before beginning to play. The audience may think the pianist is sitting passively, waiting patiently, but in fact the tempo memory wheels are smoking, turning furiously in his brain.

In an instrumental piece, things are no different. There may be fast string crossings, consecutive downbows, quick shifts from arco to pizzicato, wind passages across a break, rat-a-tat tonguing from a brass instrument—we will encounter many of these in the next chapter. These are the equivalent of text in this nonvocal arena. Again, if the pianist has the responsibility of setting the next tempo, the instant a movement or a piece ends, he downloads the stored imprint, hears it, hears it again, checks, hears it again, and begins with confidence.

Some of the most challenging pieces for tempo calculation and imprinting are those with "empty" keyboard parts. Playing an introduction leisurely with nothing active to listen to or synchronize with is seductively simple, but it is a trap awaiting our downfall. The pianist must superimpose the selected phrase on the material as it is played in order for his partner to enter seamlessly and have "room" to negotiate everything in her distinctly non-leisurely part.

EXAMPLE 10-1 Fauré, "Le secret"

In my head I hear my partner's first phrase and pay particular attention to the second half of her first measure, where all the "action" is. I begin to play, hearing it again over my part. She breathes and enters, and because I allowed for the inaudible notes during my introduction, no bump or even the slightest change is felt in the music's flow.

The second strophe, being both higher and louder, may require a slightly different tempo. As I play the two-bar introduction to that verse, I fully imagine "Je
veux que le jour le proclame," with special attention paid to the pronunciation of
"proclame," since the initial consonants might affect the tempo. Again, doing this
allows my partner to enter unobtrusively if I've done my job well beforehand.

EXAMPLE 10-2 Brahms, "O Tod, o Tod, wie bitter bist du!"

EXAMPLE 10-2 Continued

Here is a similar example, but a far more dramatic one. The tempo marking is be-yond largo, beyond adagio—how often does one encounter the direction "Grave" in a work for voice and piano only? The enormity of the philosophy expressed here must be Brahms's motivation. And yet, after coaching this song countless times, I find that neither baritone nor pianist allows for the busy texture at the words "Der Gute Tage genug hat." Brahms accompanies these words with an al-ternating-hands figure which could seem playful, jazzy, or worse, casual; any num-ber of inappropriate things might be suggested if the tempo is not slow enough. These measures should be in the singer's head as he breathes to begin the song. Alas, he must find his pitch and summon his vocal power; thus too often tempo concerns are forgotten, and the song begins andante rather than deadly slow as requested. If this should occur, the pianist now must subtly adjust the tempo down to where it should have started, using any notes that are busier than the singer's to do so.

EXAMPLE 10-3 Brahms, Violin sonata in G, op. 78, i

A classic example of needing to "hear" the missing notes is this lovely beginning to Brahms's first sonata for violin. After only eight bars the impulses will increase from two per bar to twelve per bar. The pianist, facing a mountain of a sonata, will certainly rejoice to have these relatively easy opening measures, and thus it would be easy to begin too quickly, even for the relaxed first theme in the third bar. Silently sing the busy bars to come—have you stored them on your brain's hard drive?—and accompany the missing eighth-notes as you begin the piece.

EXAMPLE 10-4 Strauss, "Morgen!"

Be in your own world at the piano—this is an incredible gift from Strauss to all collaborators. But at the return to the tonic key in the measure preceding the singer's entrance, be sure to pre-hear your partner singing "Und morgen wird" two times as you play these four beats, eliding with her actual entrance using this text. It would be a felony to change the tempo even slightly here.

EXAMPLE 10-5 Duparc, "Phidylé"

This example would seem to be the identical situation as many of the others in this section, but the slight difference here is in the eighth measure: the voice must finish "par mille issues" with a graceful cutoff, take a good breath, and re-enter as smoothly as possible. Duparc has asked for no nuance whatsoever. It is not only the voice's initial eighth notes which the pianist must pre-hear as he begins the first bar, but the time for this difficult breath many bars later as well. I always experience this exit, the poised breath, and the re-entry several times silently before I begin.

EXAMPLE 10-6 Respighi, "Nebbie"

The Italian repertoire is not exempt from this doctrine of creating the correct tempo by using active events to come. More than halfway through this haunting song, the text "Pel grigio ciel sospinto un gemito distinto vola" appears. This is a mouthful and the singer must have space to chant this clearly, but any audible tempo flexibility would lessen the horror and fear which permeate this dark atmosphere and hold us hostage. The tempo should be unrelenting from the first measure, and only the pianist's pre-calculation can guarantee this.

In working to improve your tempo memory skills, be aware that choosing the best passage for imprinting a tempo is as important as the very act of recalling it, so choose wisely. In rehearsal you may want to change plans and select another passage as a guide if it proves to offer you more indelible and infallible information than your original choice. All of this goes on in the collaborator's brain exclusively; it is no one's business but his and should remain so.

Not as I Say, but as I Do

Certain entrances can create unnecessary difficulties due to notation. This is not to suggest that it was the composer's intention to create a problem, but the fact remains that an easy-to-hear situation becomes awkward simply because of how it looks on the page. The pianist would do well to analyze how the music actually *sounds.* He then suggests that his partner hear it that way too—not as it looks—and finally, he plays it accordingly. Not seeing the printed page with its actual notation, the audience can only hear the music as it sounds. The problem disappears, leaving in its place a friendly and expressive entrance. This analysis and facilitation are part of the collaborator's job.

EXAMPLE 10-7 Schumann, "Intermezzo"

EXAMPLE 10-8 Vaughan Williams, "In dreams"

With both of these examples there is no rhythmic context to inform the listener that the pianist's first introductory notes are off the beat. If the singer is preoccupied with hearing these as syncopation, little attention will be paid to singing the first note beautifully or creating the poetic atmosphere. In the case of the Schumann song, this first sung note is rather high and soft and has an awkward diphthong to be negotiated; in the second example, the lack of an initial consonant makes the attack trickier to manage precisely.

In neither song will the music's organization be understood by the listener until the singer is at least two notes into the first phrase. Why not perform the music as it sounds? In "Intermezzo" I simply stroke a beautiful chord three times, allowing no musical difficulty to enter the singer's world; for the English song I ask my partner to do nothing more or less than hear four identical notes and sing of how tormented he is.

EXAMPLE 10-9 Berg, "Die Nachtigall"

During the transition back to the reprise of the opening section, the changing meters of 3/4 and 4/4 can prove problematic, and the hyper-rubato style of this song exacerbates the difficulty. The right hand's highest note (B) will inevitably be played with the strongest inflection, regardless of where it is in the bar. Why not mentally move the barline and assign that B the status of a downbeat, thus making it more easily identifiable aurally for the singer? This is really how the passage sounds.

Stand Your Ground!

A special way of thinking and playing is required for accompanying florid passagework, whether instrumental or vocal. It is critical that whoever is executing the fast notes never feel rushed or crowded; there must always be time to play or sing clearly and cleanly, no matter how quick the tempo. In fact, passages will actually sound faster when we can hear everything.

Faced with fewer notes and technically easier playing than his partner, the pianist should concentrate on holding the tempo rock-n-roll steady and listening very intensely to be certain the smallest notes are heard. I find that thinking the smallest rhythmic value in my part does much to help me achieve this goal. In addition, I deny myself any feeling of relaxed, casual physicality. Everything is an action; there is no simple or automatic playing. I want to create an arena wherein my partner feels that the most demanding virtuoso stunts are possible, and I want to have this in place *before* all hell breaks loose. Knowing the upcoming technical demands, I want to communicate the certainty of success while my partner can hear and feel it easily—*not* when she is already in the midst of the taxing passagework.

EXAMPLE 10-10 Rossini, "Cruda sorte," *L'italiana in Algeri*

The coda to Isabella's entrance aria is an excellent example of all I am proposing here. For the mezzo-soprano, its first two measures are jaunty and fun to sing, whereas the next two contain an intricate passage of very fast notes. Meanwhile the accompaniment is an easy "boom-chick," left hand–right hand alternation pattern which we could do in our sleep. If the pianist is too relaxed mentally in bar two, he will inadvertently fling our heroine into bars three and four with a tempo that is marginally too fast for all the impulses she must execute in each of these bars. Of course the tempo could be quickly adjusted if unclear coloratura ensued, but this shift would advertise lack of agility on the singer's part. Steadying the accompaniment *in advance* and holding it firmly in check during the virtuoso measures will be appreciated by all who sing this aria. Imitate a conductor staring intensely at his players and forbidding them to rush.

EXAMPLE IO-II Mozart, "O zittre nicht!" *Die Zauberflöte*

There is no time for the pianist to calculate the tempo for this aria's infamous second half; only half a bar separates the mother's lament from her imperious orders for Tamino. All is not lost, however, if the tempo is too quick; the fireworks are far down the road. The crucial moment for my technique of "pre-steadying" is five measures before the scales begin. These measures are not particularly difficult for either performer, and it is even possible the soprano may wonder why the accompaniment is not being allowed to simply flow blithely along. Her curiosity will surely change to gratitude when her fast notes begin and she realizes there is time to articulate them all.

Throughout my career so many of my regular partners have programmed a great deal of music featuring florid singing and demanding maximum agility that I have had countless opportunities to use the ideas expressed here. They work. A singer may not always succeed with every brilliant passage, but if virtuosity eludes her it will hopefully not be because of my failure to plan ahead or to create and hold a steady tempo.

Mixed Messages

Pianists are normally very proficient at multi-tasking. Playing different amounts of notes per beat simultaneously is something we encounter while quite young, often in the second or third year of piano lessons. I suspect instrumentalists share this early acquaintance as well, playing, as they do, in youth orchestras and chamber ensembles. Singers, on the other hand, come to formal music lessons later than their colleagues and often have limited keyboard proficiency. Negotiating two rhythmic patterns at once will not be something they have often or regularly experienced. They may not encounter repertoire requiring two notes against three or three against four until their college or conservatory studies. As collaborators we must be especially sensitive to this possibility, never assuming they will have the same automatic reflex as we do. It is actually easier to do both tasks than to execute only the part with fewer notes.

The following advice is needed, therefore, but only when the voice has the smaller number of impulses per beat than the piano; the opposite is not at all a problem, for it is entirely the pianist's job to time the longer note unit correctly. In my experience, singers divide into two groups when facing this rhythmic issue. Half of them will practice hearing their cross-rhythm and succeed by feeling the large beat; the other half will ignore the large beat and manage by simply inserting their own impulse between the appropriate smaller notes in the piano part. Regardless of which method a singer is using—and it might be better *not* to inquire anyway—the pianist must take care to play the most expansive version of the notes in question. There must be adequate room for the singer's "foreign" impulse to intrude. Further, he must identify which of his smaller notes triggers the vocal note to be inserted and must make sure it is audible. This is not to suggest adding an accent that might sound inappropriate, but rather giving just enough clarity to a note we might otherwise ignore so that the singer can use it as a guide.

EXAMPLE 10-12 Duparc, "Elégie"

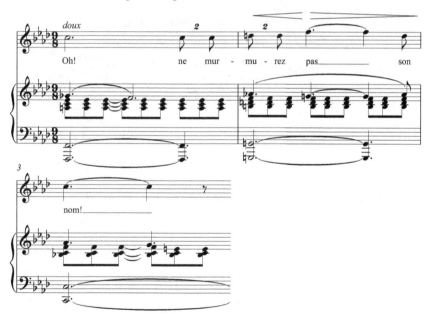

EXAMPLE 10-13 Dvorak, "Má písen zas mi láskou zní"

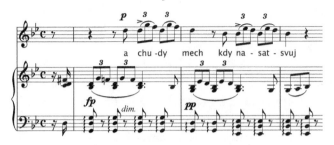

EXAMPLE 10-14 Fauré, "En sourdine"

These are three examples of moments of cross-rhythms in the standard song literature. The pianist must *always* be physically and mentally aware of all his impulses in any beat where the singer behaves at odds with his part. The Dvorak example is particularly nasty, because the singer's inserted note follows a rest.

Draining the Tank

We pay so much attention to monitoring the breathing of our vocal partners. We make certain they have time for an adequate intake of oxygen, and if we have moving notes in the accompaniment we are continually concerned with making sure the singer reaches the end of each phrase. To behave otherwise would seem "un-collaborative," not suited to vocal accompanying at all. But very occasionally—believe it or not—our job is to ensure that the singer runs out of breath. Before you think me insane, let me elucidate.

Faced with a verbal phrase that ought to be in one breath but where that is simply not possible, the singer chooses a place to breathe but camouflages her "shortcoming" as an intentional artistic decision, not something apologetic or unplanned. The most successful disguises and the most believable breaths are those involuntary responses to being out of air. Thus the goal becomes using up all her breath, and here the pianist is her best ally. By playing slowly enough that the singer's breath becomes absolutely necessary, we can make this phrasing seem to be our joint preference as well as the only interpretation possible.

● EXAMPLE 10-15 Donaudy, "O del mio amato ben"

This song of lost love makes no apologies for its heart-on-sleeve expression. At its final cadence, if the pianist ritards sufficiently, the singer will be forced to breathe dramatically before "senza il mio ben" ("without my beloved"). Simply obeying the breath instruction from the composer without physiologically needing to breathe will always seem artificial, shallow, and foreign to the raw emotion of this piece.

EXAMPLE 10-16 Berg, "Schilflied"

In this second of Berg's seven early songs, most singers require a breath between an adjective and the noun it modifies (lovely . . . singing) in the song's last sentence. The only way to be convincing with this situation is to create a highly emotional moment, a moment when grammar ceases to matter. Since the accompaniment controls the progress of the music here, it is easy to run the singer completely out of breath and make her breath a credible necessity.

I hasten to emphasize that this special treatment of the singer's air supply might occur once in two hundred songs or arias. The performers would use it only if the composer should specifically ask for an unusual breath or as a last resort when normal interpretation and phrasing are not possible. It should be used sparingly, and most important, it must be a conscious decision on the part of the pianist to employ this technique, once he knows his partner intends to breathe where the text would not ordinarily call for it.

Short *and* Sweet

In addition to deciding how best to copy the orchestra's sounds *and* remain comfortable, it is sometimes necessary to abbreviate extended orchestral passages, be they introductions, interludes, or postludes. This situation is most often encountered in an audition, master class, or similar situation where the soloist stands more in the spotlight than usual. This never would happen with song or sonata repertoire, but I would say it is an inherent and logical part of the collaborator's job to recognize the appropriateness of cutting orchestral measures where the soloist is absent, and then, of course, to determine what to exclude.

One hears pianists offering only the last few measures before the soloist enters as their "cut version" of the introduction. Yes, doing this saves lots of time, but I feel that the integrity of the excerpt—already compromised by the decision to cut—is further disrespected. I much prefer to begin the experience as the composer wishes and then do any cutting *inside* the too-long orchestral passage. This preservation of the opening material can also help the soloist to imagine the atmosphere of a complete integral performance and be genuinely inspired as intended.

EXAMPLE 10-17 Mozart, "Porgi, amor, qualche ristoro," *Le Nozze di Figaro*

EXAMPLE 10-17 Continued

We meet the lady of the house for the first time in this aria which opens the second act of *Figaro*. The listener learns many things about her during this long orchestral prelude. Mozart, the psychologist, shows us the Countess's conflicting feelings. To begin only two or three measures before the singer, as is so often done, shows us only one part of her psyche. I would recommend preserving the majesty of the opening chords, the imperial quality of the forte double-dotted phrase, and the touching vulnerability of the music just preceding the soprano's entrance. Yes, we have used up ten or fifteen additional seconds, but the reward of a richer inspiration is certainly worth the time lost.

EXAMPLE 10-18 R. Strauss, "Wie du warst!" *Der Rosenkavalier*

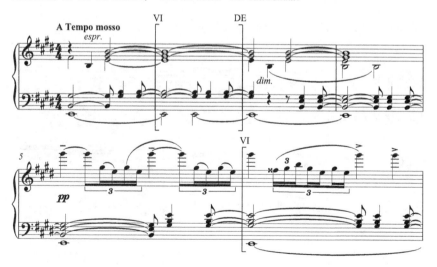

EXAMPLE 10-18 Continued

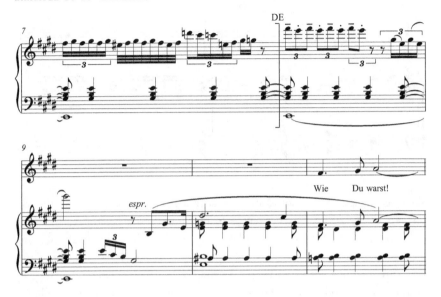

There are two elements in this introduction: birds announcing daybreak, and warm, langorous "bedroom" harmonies. Both are essential. The former puts an end, alas, to the latter. Make your cut in the middle of this orchestral passage. The example above shows one possible cut, honoring both musical characters.

EXAMPLE 10-19 Bach, "Mache dich, mein Herze rein," *St. Matthew Passion*

EXAMPLE 10-19 Continued

In order to devise a shortened orchestral passage and remain respectful to the opening and closing measures, it may be necessary for the pianist to assume the role of composer very temporarily. Doing so may strike the reader as heretical—tampering with the great masters, for heaven's sake! Personally, I would choose the misdemeanor of creative practicality over the felony of inappropriate long-windedness.

With excerpted operatic arias, there is yet another decision which must be made by the pianist—with the singer's cooperation and input, of course. This concerns where to begin. Two of the previous examples are from numbered operas or oratorios, and therefore the composer has chosen the beginning of the excerpt for us. We may or may not shorten the introduction, as was discussed above, but the first measure is clearly designated. By the middle of the nineteenth century, however, a score often had no table of contents, for whole through-composed scenes began to be the norm. The decision of where to begin the introduction to an aria therefore falls to the performers.

Some arias evolve out of the material immediately preceding them so that the seam is virtually inaudible. The feelings grow and blossom into an aria. Others make their initial statement by way of violent contrast with the foregoing music; in these cases, the singer's feelings perform an about-face, often heightening the aria's theatricality as it begins. The composer has calculated these diverse impacts, and we can preserve this design by choosing creative places to begin. If you are using a published anthology of operatic arias, *please* don't be a slave to where the editor has suggested you begin and end. Have a look at the score of the complete opera and note how the excerpted aria is "born," how it fits or doesn't fit into the music surrounding it. In performance of the aria, don't waste time needlessly playing extraneous bars, but do spend the time necessary to simulate the conditions as they exist in the opera proper. Both your audience and your singer—perhaps you yourself as well—will be more inspired, I assure you.

EXAMPLE 10-20 Puccini, "Sola, perduta, abbandonata," *Manon Lescaut*

Most people choose to begin this powerful aria with the five loud dramatic orchestra chords immediately preceding it. These take only a few seconds, and *ecco!* we are in the midst of Manon's desperation. What intensifies her pain, however, is a tune heard several measures earlier when the opera's love theme is played in the orchestra. This theme was born when life was carefree, when romance with Des Grieux was at its height. If the orchestra is playing it, we can assume Manon is recalling it and feeling it again. Hearing this reminiscence motivates and justifies the aria, even heightening its bittersweet effect. I cannot imagine beginning the excerpt elsewhere.

EXAMPLE 10-21 Verdi, "Stride la vampa," *Il trovatore*

EXAMPLE 10-22 Verdi, "E strano, è strano," *La traviata*

Here are similar situations, but they work in exactly the opposite way of the previous example. Azucena's first notes are heard in a demented, pianissimo aria. The ghostly dynamic and folksy simplicity of her singing is in direct, calculated opposition to the preceding music, the famous "Anvil Chorus." Thus quite a racket is followed immediately by the eeriest quiet. Without a bit of the loud chorus, we cannot really appreciate what soft is. Similarly, Violetta's great scene begins unaccompanied, following a rousing goodbye from all her party guests. The full orchestra—particularly the brass—makes the measures preceding her first notes a perfect foil for her quiet musing. Most anthologies offer the pianist the suggestion of one simple, generic chord or worse, nothing at all. The pianist must create enough noise to exploit the silence that follows.

Eleven

Is There Life after Singers?

It comes as no surprise to anyone that my own career has centered principally on the vocal repertoire; indeed, if my name is known at all, it is for anything and everything that has to do with singers. But I hasten to add proudly that my student years were equally divided between partnering instruments and voices, and with equal amounts of enthusiasm and personal reward on my part. Accompanying the classes of luminary Jascha Heifetz for two years not only was thrilling (and intimidating), it has proved to have been nothing less than a cornerstone of my artistic development, certainly as much as any of my endeavors in the worlds of opera or song. Indeed, one of the benefits of becoming a professor and working within a fine music school has been the reactivation of this instrumental repertoire in my daily activities, both performing it myself and helping my students to understand and succeed in this branch of collaboration too.

For those of us who spend the majority of our time with singers, creating perfect ensemble with an instrument can seem inexplicably difficult at first. Gone are the obvious aids or subconscious cues which the text affords us. With no consonant to tell us that the next impulse is imminent, we can easily feel totally at sea and begin to doubt our capacity for ensemble altogether. This happens to me at almost every first rehearsal with an instrumental partner. With strings, at least the bow is a kind of conductor, a visual aid for much of what we need, but with winds and brass, less is outwardly visible and initially our confidence can be completely shattered. We may feel disoriented, embarrassed, and all too quickly convinced that we are incapable of being perfectly together with anyone at all. These frightening feelings are short-lived, however, and with just a bit of extra patience, instincts and intuitions will "kick in."

Because words are absent, it is particularly important for the pianist to make use of visual information. With most wind and brass partners as well as some cellists, we can keep our gaze forward or perhaps slightly to the right of the music rack of the piano, just as we do with singers, more or less maintaining our accustomed keyboard orientation. With violin, viola, and some cellists who prefer to sit to the right of the piano, we must use peripheral vision or turn our heads to the right more than just occasionally to see the necessary visual cues. This alteration of our physical focus can upset our applecart significantly, create a temporary loss of keyboard sense, and seriously threaten our accuracy. It is *essential* to identify events when visual cues are our only guide for perfect ensemble, and as a matter of course to practice those events alone *in advance of rehearsing with our partner,* so that the disorientation inherent in our turning to the right becomes quasi-familiar and not more than minimally disruptive to our playing well.

When do these moments that must be visually cued occur? How does the pianist identify them? The simple answer: when there are no moving notes in either player's part to serve as an audible guide to the music's progress. Even after countless rehearsals or years of partnership, it is still impossible for one performer to be truly *inside* the mind of the other; if there are no intervening notes between two impulses that the performers must strike together, our eyes are all we have for information. With vocal music, consonant sounds or diphthongs can announce the next note, but obviously here in this world of instrumental repertoire we have no such convenience. To reiterate: a pianist preparing for an instrumental collaboration must identify these musical moments requiring visual cues, analyze how she will need to behave physically, and practice, always assuming the worst. If rehearsals surprise us and ensemble is more easily achieved than was expected, so much the better; at least she will not be found wanting or inexperienced.

Working with Strings

Since so much of the instrumental repertoire is for piano and strings, it is important to become as familiar with the physical side of playing these instruments as is possible for a keyboard player. Leaving collaboration aside for a moment, an unexpected and very welcome by-product of spending time with strings is the visible manifestation they afford of things which pianists can only suggest. Legato pianism depends on illusion, thanks to the decaying and percussive nature of the instrument, whereas real legato is naturally and beautifully demonstrated by the bow. On the keyboard, playing an interval can amount to simply moving a few inches to the right or left, or worse, an intellectualization of how an interval feels. On a violin or cello the cost of steps and intervals is shown clearly by the fingers and wrist. Working with a string player gives us a physical role model for so many of our musical aspirations which at best can only be simulated at the piano. In addition, never lose touch with the bow; keep it within your sight at all times. It is the best of conductors, showing us attacks, releases, phrasing, as well as the music's fundamental attitudes as interpreted by our partner.

To Pluck, to Bow

EXAMPLE 11-1 Brahms, Violin sonata in G, op. 78, i

EXAMPLE 11-2 Brahms, Cello sonata in F, op. 99, ii

Fast changes in and out of pizzicato and arco must be taken into account when you are planning tempi, rubato, and phrasing. The player must have time to adjust the right hand and the bow more or less comfortably. If the pianist sees her partner scrambling, and it is *not* a virtuoso perpetual motion etude, then the pianist must change the execution of her intervening material during this articulation shift.

The Retaken Bow

As I said earlier, phrasing becomes visible with strings. Nowhere is this more true than on those infrequent occasions when a string player chooses to retake the bow. Finishing a phrase and beginning the next in the same direction requires a special gesture, one that should never fail to register immediately on the pianist's radar screen. I love this bowing; it is nothing less than visible breathing and the best guide to phrasing I know. A collaborative pianist must *feel* this bowing in her own arms and hands in order to be as complete a physical ally as possible.

EXAMPLE II-3 Beethoven, Cello sonata in A, op. 69, i

EXAMPLE II-4 Beethoven, Violin sonata in c-minor, op. 30, #2, ii

Dealing with Chords

EXAMPLE 11-5 Schumann, Piano concerto, i

EXAMPLE 11-6 Beethoven, Violin sonata in a minor, op. 47

EXAMPLE 11-7 Mozart, Violin sonata in B-flat, K.454, i

EXAMPLE II-8 Debussy, Violin sonata, iii

EXAMPLE II-9 Strauss, Violin sonata, iii

EXAMPLE II-10 Brahms, Violin sonata in d-minor, op. 108, i

Above is an assortment of events all sharing the same effect: whether notated as grace notes, arpeggios, or single chords, none of these examples is played as one impulse. In repertoire for the piano, notated bass grace notes almost always come before the beat, and notated rolled chords are initiated so as to end on the beat, irrespective of the direction of the arpeggio. When the two impulses are not notated, distance and hand size dictate if and how the player elects to divide a chord. For the string player, while some chords of three notes can be played as one impulse, this is never possible with four-note chords. A string player playing a four-note chord will need to "break" it into two parts. In almost every case the bottom of the chord would be played before the beat. The top, or the completion of the chord, will therefore be on the beat. Occasionally, primarily with contemporary scores, a player will be instructed or choose to break his chord in a downward direction. Regardless of the direction, however, if a pianist has something simultaneous to play with this chord, it should be synchronized by being played with the second and last element of the chord.

But who manages this synchronization? For once, it is not automatically the pianist's responsibility. In the first three examples above, there is more than adequate time before the two-part impulse, so the string chord-player (or pianist in the first example) can "borrow" time from the previous note or silence, initiate the chord early, and complete it on time, allowing his partner at the piano (or the orchestra) to proceed simply and without any concern. The last three examples in the list, however, have too many notes and too little time before the chord to be broken; there is no time available for borrowing, as in the first situations. Now the responsibility for perfect ensemble shifts to the pianist, who must postpone the beat if the synchronization is to be ideal. This situation is completely analogous to its vocal equivalent of too many consonants and too little time, discussed in depth in chapter 3. I make it a point to mark four-note chords for my string partners in my own part—*before I begin to learn a piece.* I integrate any necessary delay into my practicing from the outset, and it becomes the only way I can play the piece. I am not surprised at our first rehearsal, and my partner is comfortable from the outset too.

Sexy Shifts, Juicy Fingering

For a string player to perform the romantic repertoire without incorporating an expressive use of his left hand would be tantamount to eating spaghetti with no sauce—not a culinary pleasure, to be sure. Some of these effects are physical necessities: string changes, for example; the application of others is simply a sensuous choice. Both romanticize, humanize, and personalize the music immeasurably.

EXAMPLE 11-11 Strauss, Violin sonata, i

EXAMPLE 11-12 Brahms, Violin sonata in A, op. 100, ii

EXAMPLE 11-13 Franck, Violin sonata, ii

A pianist cannot understand how these moments actually *feel* firsthand—more's the pity!—but if one is listening intently, these effects and any additional time they require are easily heard and appreciated. These are hyper-romantic soundbites; synchronize with them by experiencing them vicariously. Never make your string partner feel apologetic for taking time and exploiting the glory of what his instrument can say.

Using the Left Hand

EXAMPLE 11-14 Franck, Violin sonata, i

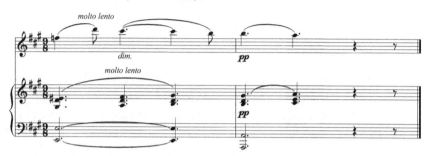

EXAMPLE 11-15 Bartok, Contrasts, ii

EXAMPLE 11-16 Strauss, Violin sonata, ii

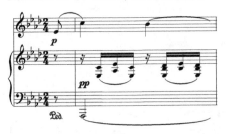

Normally the bow tells us all we need to know. We observe the right arm's prepa-ration and probably do not need to see the actual moment of contact with the string, much as we would follow a conductor's upbeat and know all that is wanted for the downbeat which follows. However, there are moments when we must syn-chronize with a note in the string part *without* a bow change. The only possible life-line for ensemble in these instances is the string player's left hand. You can predict this necessity by first identifying moments when no intervening music informs you of when to play. Then, looking at the string line, in the presence of a slur you learn that the bow will not conduct you for this one-on-one event. Practice look-ing at an imaginary fingerboard before going to your first rehearsal.

Page Turns

If you think negotiating pages without a turner is difficult for a pianist, imagine the disruption for a violinist or violist. Their entire physical attitude is far more disturbed than ours, creating a vulnerability at these moments which no one could envy. Be a compassionate collaborator; if your music during these "free fall" mo-ments can afford to lend your partner some comfort and remove even a bit of stress or worry, don't be guilty of insensitivity or rigidity. How will you know they need your empathy? Look to your right!

Woodwinds and Brass

Collaborating with winds and brass has its own specific issues, perhaps fewer in number than strings present, but in a way more challenging since the visual man-ifestation of both the music and the soloist's intentions which we have seen to be so helpful in the string repertoire is for the most part missing here.

  Much of the excellent playing in these two instrumental families has nothing to do with keys or fingers but is managed by the lips, the tongue, the teeth, and, of course, the lungs—all fairly invisible to any pianist. I always encourage my partners in this repertoire to be physical enough for me to "read" them with assurance. If their body language continues to be insufficient, the consistent lack of perfect ensemble will soon wage its own campaign for their doing a bit more. All we have, after all, are cues given with their breaths, with their instruments as quasi-batons, and, we would hope, with subtle but clear arm and upper body motions; these will do the job, once we have learned to interpret the body language of each of our wind or brass partners.

Wind Specifics

EXAMPLE 11-17 Schubert, Trock'ne Blumen Variations, var. #1

EXAMPLE 11-18 Reinecke, Flute sonata, op. 167, iii

Flutes seem to breathe more often and more quickly than all other winds, reminding me of frequent snacking between meals. As you study their scores, try to predict where these "emergency" breaths may occur, adding only micro-seconds to the flow of the music but definitely influencing our work at the piano when we have notes to be synchronized. The lower register of the flute seems to use more air less efficiently, and one can expect even more frequent breaths, as in the second of the examples above.

EXAMPLE 11-19 Schumann, Romance for oboe and piano, op. 94, #2

EXAMPLE 11-19 Continued

EXAMPLE 11-20 Debussy, Rhapsody #1 for clarinet

EXAMPLE II-20 Continued

Some oboists are proficient at circular breathing, but I am not convinced that this aids the music, since it can potentially remove the need to phrase. That unique trick aside, we obviously need to be as sensitive to winds' breath needs as we would to any singer's. These two examples from the standard repertoire will tax any oboist or clarinetist to the utmost. The absence of rests in the wind parts is an automatic visual flag for the pianist. This is sure and certain information that regardless of the tempo, the music must give and take, flowing during their playing and flexing during their breathing (and swallowing) to allow the wind soloist to survive.

EXAMPLE II-21 Schubert, Der Hirt auf dem Felsen

Schubert gave the clarinet this masterpiece, but it is a gift with strings attached. Its dozen final measures end the piece with a flourish, but they are not trouble-free. It is not the speed that is the problem here—we all know how quickly this instrument can perform cascades of notes; rather it is the crossing and re-crossing of the clarinet's register breaks, which, if not done gingerly and carefully, can produce extra-musical sounds we never want to hear. Most pianists, if I am any example, will not be conversant with these invisible mechanics; we must inform ourselves in rehearsal conversations. These technical pitfalls will be common to all players of this instrument, of course, and future partners will reap the benefits of our educating ourselves.

I include this brilliant postlude as a classic example of technically awkward in-strumental passagework accompanied by technically simple material for the piano. The collaborator's job here is to remove the pressure the clarinetist surely feels as he confronts ending the piece without mishap. Be sure that the off-beats in the right hand are not played as simple reactions to the beats in the left. Pretend these bars are difficult for the keyboard too. If the pianist thinks four impulses in each measure, no sense of haste can harass the soloist. Consider this a first cousin anal-ogy to my remarks in chapter 10 about accompanying coloratura passages for voice.

An Instrumental Coda

Tuning Up

Be sure at the outset to learn each instrumental partner's preferences for tuning. So many methods are in practice, one could not state any rules as to which pitches or which octaves are desired. Ask too if, during a multi-movement work, your partner might want to re-tune, and how will you know this is the case? Nothing does the trick like friendly conversation in rehearsal, and if you are lucky enough to be busy with many instrumental engagements at once, *write things down!* There is no shame in guaranteeing success and mental comfort for everyone involved.

Without question the notes you play for tuning should be the softest in your entire repertoire. Surely it will come as no surprise that the whole mechanical pro-cess of tuning is not music and is not appreciated by the audience. Tuning should remain as brief and unobtrusive to the performance as humanly possible. My fa-vorite partners tune offstage; we simply walk on and begin.

Vulnerable Moments

Both violinist and clarinetist have to change instruments *during* the music in Bartok's "Contrasts," and in many pieces in the brass repertoire different mutes are inserted and removed quickly during the music's flow. Changes such as these create zones of potential accidents; the soloist may have everything on his mind except the music. Never assume that all is well; be prepared to assist musically or visually, confirming the soloist's next entrance after such a change. As was stated previously, never let your instrumental partner completely leave your field of vision. Your concern will be appreciated, even if your emergency measures are never needed.

Singing and Playing—Again!

In chapter 2 I presented my ironclad credo that a collaborator must always be capable of singing and playing simultaneously. In this chapter dealing with instrumental partnership, I state this again without compromise or apology. Obviously the instrumental part will contain much that is unsingable; the music will be too high or low, too fast or slow; intervals will be unreachable vocally, or the music will be too dissonant or atonal to reproduce comfortably with an untrained voice. Singing all the correct pitches in the correct registers is not only impossible, it is completely unimportant. What is crucial is threefold: simulating the shape of your partner's part, suggesting the required articulation, and accounting for each and every impulse that is played.

These three requirements can be met with any method that works. Help yourself to nonsense syllables if they help with articulation. Sketch the shapes with some personally contrived combination of sprechstimme, chanting, and classical scat, and be purposely unconcerned with pitch. In the string and wind repertoires you will frequently accompany lightning fast virtuoso passages, and your ears will have to learn to listen for *all* the notes. Nothing will prepare you for this better than executing—in any way you can—these "impossible" passages yourself. People eavesdropping on your practice may think you ridiculous or even demented, but any foolish feeling you experience is easily justified by the confidence and security you acquire by putting yourself through this process.

In conclusion let me say that much as I love vocal music, I am also mindful of its inherent limitations: songs and arias are generally the smallest musical forms a composer can choose; they are written for an instrument with a comparatively small range, often limited power, and only moderate agility. As collaborators we need the most sweeping overview possible of all the repertoire if we are to make fully informed choices for any one segment of it. Studying instrumental works immediately extends our concept of what form can be; it demands larger thinking and larger playing over longer arches. Often as demanding as music for solo piano, the instrumental repertoire can only improve the collaborator's facility and technique. Finally, a wonderful exchange of assets can take place if a pianist shuttles back and forth from vocal to instrumental repertoire. Few collaborators will earn their living equally in both worlds, but all would benefit greatly from this double acquaintance.

TWELVE

In Conclusion: A Pep Talk

It is almost a cliché that any text about collaborative piano will discuss the thanklessness, the inequality, and the lack of appreciation inherent in this choice of career. I cannot argue with all of that; those negatives do indeed exist to some degree, but I am also very mindful of how far we have traveled in this profession and how rewarding it can be.

For those of us whose careers as collaborative pianists began in the last third of the twentieth century, life has become more and more gratifying with each passing year. It is important to remember that only one hundred years ago accompanists (the only word in use back then) played concerts behind screens so as not to interfere with the adulation of the Star. Often pianists' names were not even listed on programs, nor did a single collaborator have any reputation beyond the small stable of his regular employers. There is no need to be concerned with pronouns in writing about pianists in that period, for women had no opportunity whatsoever to pursue this specialty, much less to be appreciated. Piano introductions were routinely slashed to a measure or two, and postludes, even when played in their entirety, were inaudible because of immediate applause for the soloist.

None of this remains in effect today. At least two dozen academic institutions in North America teach collaboration as a specific curriculum. When it comes to concerts, programs and posters advertise collaborators in bold print, the lids of pianos are fully raised on many an occasion, and applause on stage is usually taken by duos, not divas. Finally—as hard as it is to imagine—even books are published solely about the art of collaborative playing! The formerly unsung hero is singing out loudly and clearly these days . . . but never *too* loud, of course.

If there is a down side to this relatively recent improvement in the collaborator's life, it is that with increased awareness of who we are comes increased sensitivity to what we are actually doing at the piano. Too much partnering on a high level is heard and enjoyed these days for uninformed work to be considered acceptable.

Whereas synchronization might have been enough a century ago, it is the bare minimum today.

First and foremost, this is no longer a profession for pianists without significant technical facility; obviously one cannot begin to approach working with others until the prerequisite of fluency at the instrument is securely in place. Particularly, though not exclusively, in dealing with string and wind partners, instrumental virtuosity has reached a high threshold which must be matched at the piano without exception. As we have seen with orchestral accompaniments, a pianist needs to know what makes him or her comfortable, and must have enough keyboard sense to be extremely creative in substituting difficult but playable gestures for entirely unpianistic ones.

With vocal repertoire, I find that today's singers, whether still in training or busy celebrities, react immediately and positively to a creative and informed accompaniment. Once having experienced this, they are reluctant to settle for generic or unimaginative partnering. When it comes to breathing and phrasing, they may not always know precisely *why* it is comfortable to sing with one pianist and not with another, but the difference is palpable to each of them, and they soon become intent on hiring someone who is in touch with their physical process.

With command of the instrument and a special aptitude for ensemble in place, there still remain other skills which any professional collaborator must have. Chief among these would have to be sight-reading. Make no mistake: a talent for sight-reading is no barometer of musicality; there are very artistic musicians who cannot read well at all, as well as hopelessly untalented souls who are champions at sight-reading. For a collaborative pianist, however, the ability to grasp things quickly and deliver an unpolished perhaps but very acceptable reading for a rehearsal, audition, or lesson is essential. Life for a successful collaborator is life in the fast lane, which would be impossible without this special skill. I hasten to point out that talent for sight-reading *must* be coupled with an appetite for learning a piece thoroughly and carefully, or the first reading will be the best performance that pianist ever achieves. Let us not confuse a clever coordination ability with real artistry. Only the presence of both makes a professional career possible.

I am often asked about transposition. People wonder if it is true that singers may ask for something in a new key while you are both waiting in the wings just moments before a recital. I can honestly say that this has never happened to me. Requests for transposing songs have come as late as one or two days before a concert, but never later. I would consider transposition a footnote to the list of associated skills collaborators often need, nothing more. It is a wonderful skill to have, and it does improve the more one does it, but today there is a great deal of technology that can handle this feat for the pianist, leaving him or her time for other chores.

With Baroque music, both vocal and instrumental, and bel canto repertoire for the voice, we will probably be expected to invent ornaments for our partners, as well as to realize the accompaniments of various pieces scored only for figured bass. More than occasionally, a singer wants to do a folksong or a popular song, perhaps as an encore, and it may fall to the pianist to compose an arrangement. These are not essential skills, but they add to who we are as musicians, and they can quickly increase the demand for our services as well as the esteem in which we are held. Less definable but critically important for the collaborator are "people" skills. Mastering everything this book presents would count for nothing if a conversation backstage undermined someone's confidence or if a chance remark in rehearsal implied lack of discretion or disrespect for one's partner.

Without losing our own self-respect, we must be now disciplinarians, now psychologists, now diplomats, now patient listeners, now mommy and daddy—the list of our roles is endless. Before a performance we may be quaking with nerves, but our role as collaborators is to inspire confidence by displaying self-confidence. As repertoire is being planned, we may have to steer a partner away from something we know is inappropriate, but if we do our job, the risky piece will be changed, and without hard feelings or critical remarks. The list goes on and on.

Without a love of other people and a sincere desire to help them do their best, collaboration cannot exist. There is a great deal of giving to be done; the gift to ourselves is the elation, the pride we take in being indispensable to our partner's success. This giving is not easy for everyone; it is essential nevertheless.

So with all these requirements, why would anyone be foolish enough to pursue this super-specialized, very demanding branch of music-making? As was said at the beginning of this chapter, there remain some less than ideal aspects of the profession that may never change. When it comes to wealth or fame, no collaborator can compete with a soloist, no matter how successful he or she is. If these are your goals and priorities, collaborative piano is not for you. If you experience no particular pride or excitement when accompanying someone, or if failure as a soloist has led you to try this field, then think again, collaborative piano is surely not your "thing."

If, on the other hand, you love voice or violin and want to be part of that world but you can't sing or fiddle, working with those instruments from the keyboard may be just what you're looking for. If you enjoy telling stories at the piano, or turning the Steinway into a wonderful orchestral color machine, collaboration would be one way to go about doing so. If the high voltage of opera is your passion, if your coaching leads a soloist to a more memorable performance of a concerto, if you are a poetry and language devotee, and if, above all, you love company as you seek expression, I'm fairly confident you have the aptitude for collaborative work. Collaborators are certainly the most versatile of all musicians, and as a happy consequence, we will always be the last to starve.

I have had the audacity to call this handbook complete. I ask the reader's indulgence; perhaps I was swayed by the catchy alliteration of the title. Obviously there are many points I have inadvertently ignored, consciously avoided, or simply forgotten. I can think of several as I write these lines, and I will hear of them soon, no doubt. Apologies aside, however, I feel that a great many of the tools necessary to be an excellent partner can be found herein. Much is expected of us, but we must expect even more of ourselves. There is almost an overabundance of information to be taken onboard, digested, and implemented before one can feel he or she is collaborating in every sense of the word. I began this text by asking what collaboration was; now I ask, "What is *not* collaboration?" The task is undoubtedly daunting, but I can assure you that the reward is immense.

Index

Italics indicate pages with musical examples.